Otherwise

Essays

By Julie Marie Wade

 AUTUMN
HOUSE PRESS

Pittsburgh, PA

Cover and Book Design: Melissa Dias-Mandoly
Cover Art: Highsmith, Carol M, photographer. *Colorful Historic Motel, Wildwood, New Jersey*. Photograph. Wildwood, New Jersey, 2006. Library of Congress: Carol M. Highsmith Archive. https://www.loc.gov/item/2010630067/.

Grateful acknowledgment is made for permission to reprint the following:

Robert Creeley, "The Flower" ["I think I grow tensions"] from *The Collected Poems of Robert Creeley 1945–1975*. Copyright © 1962 by Robert Creeley. Reprinted with the permission of The Permissions Company, LLC on behalf of the Estate of Robert Creeley.

The lines from "Splittings". Copyright © 2016 by the Adrienne Rich Literary Trust. Copyright (c) 1978 by W. W. Norton & Company, Inc, from COLLECTED POEMS: 1950--2012 by Adrienne Rich. Used by permission of W. W. Norton & Company, Inc.

Library of Congress Cataloging-in-Publication Data

Names: Wade, Julie Marie, author.
Title: Otherwise : essays / by Julie Marie Wade.
Description: Pittsburgh : Autumn House Press, 2023.
Identifiers: LCCN 2023023526 (print) | LCCN 2023023527 (ebook) | ISBN 9781637680728 (paperback) | ISBN 9781637680759 (epub)
Subjects: LCSH: Wade, Julie Marie. | LCGFT: Essays.
Classification: LCC PS3623.A345 O84 2023 (print) | LCC PS3623.A345 (ebook) | DDC 814/.6 [B]--dc23/eng/20230609
LC record available at https://lccn.loc.gov/2023023526
LC ebook record available at https://lccn.loc.gov/2023023527

This book was printed in the United States on acid-free paper that meets the international standards of permanent books intended for purchase by libraries.

Autumn House Press is a nonprofit corporation whose mission is the publication and promotion of poetry and other fine literature. The press gratefully acknowledges support

from individual donors, public and private foundations, and government agencies. This book was supported, in part, by the Greater Pittsburgh Arts Council through its Allegheny Arts Revival Grant and the Pennsylvania Council on the Arts, a state agency funded by the Commonwealth of Pennsylvania.

For Angie Griffin
It always had to do with you

Contents

Otherwise

Meditation 32

old.

Once upon a time, there was a girl who was not an orphan tended by a woman who was not a nanny in a red brick house that could never be, by any calisthenics of imagination, a castle—though it did have a view of the sea.

That girl, sitting at the table, was me. That woman, standing by the stove, was my mother.

Back then, we lived in the late splendor of catalogs. Everything we ever wanted could be found on a glossy page. Locate the little white letter in the upper right corner, then call and place your order.

I liked to linger in *Lingerie*, with my scissors and my paste and my tablet of bright construction paper. These were old catalogs, mine to cut and alter. My mother stirred a pot of something frothy and said, "Pack a suitcase." This was only pretend. She wanted me to choose the clothes I would take on the trip that comes after the wedding.

If the man was there, the man who was every day less my savior and more my father, he would fill a glass with water and lean beside the sink. "Did someone order a honeymoon salad?" I never got it. I shook my head. Then, he'd chuckle—"Lettuce alone!"

I noticed, over time, the faces of women in the catalog. There were not many of them, so the same woman wore garment after garment, sometimes with her hair down or her lipstick lightly blotted. One face I loved—the dark curls, the pert nose, the creamy complexion. She posed in nightgowns, pajamas, matching bras and panties. Once, I found her in a black-lace bodysuit. Though it seemed transparent, nothing was visible beneath it. I expected a glimpse of her real body, but she had none. She was like a doll arranged on a low chaise lounge: her elbow bent by someone else, a smile painted across her lips, her bright eyes unblinking.

"Have you found what you'll wear on your wedding night?" My mother leaned across the counter as I tore the page free and trimmed its edges.

"*This*," I said, triumphant.

"That's a little racy," she murmured. "Why don't you try again?"

blue.

One of my earliest memories is of a wedding: It is blurry in that way memories are before they contain coherent narratives. Summer, I think, because my skin is warm. I wear a white eyelet dress with a blue sash that matches the blue ribbon tied around my white Easter bonnet. My parents are there—my mother in a long skirt, my father in suit and tie. We sit in chairs on the lawn, and someone rolls a carpet down the makeshift aisle. A woman with hair like a silver curtain strums the strings of a harp.

I cannot conjure precisely the bride and groom, the minister's deep voice or his lavish robes, the boy who bears the rings. Two girls, not much older than I, scatter petals from small woven baskets. My mother squeezes my hand. I study everyone's shoes. In the distance, a little dog paces behind a fence, waiting for the dancing to begin.

I think in the way of thoughts before they are tethered to words, parcels made tidy with knowing. One gist, folded into a bow—*this is the most important thing I could ever do.*

old.

I have cut three wedding gowns from the catalog and smoothed them onto thick sheets of paper. My mother reviews them, remarks on the gown she likes best.

"And when will this wedding take place?"

"Christmastime," I say. "There should be snow. We may have to go to the mountains."

"The best time for a wedding is spring or summer. Your father and I were married in August."

"But my bridesmaids will wear velvet," I explain. "Red velvet dresses with furry white pouches to keep their hands warm." I have seen these before in a film.

"How will they carry their flowers?" She is testing me now.

"White roses," I say, "pinned to their pretty lapels."

I thought the wedding was a fashion show, a commercial for the marriage.

But what was a marriage? I did not know.

borrowed.

It was a treasure hunt, but we always meant to put everything back. A distant cousin was getting married at a distant house. I fell asleep on the car ride there. When I saw my closer cousin, she was ready. She had her mother's old valise—leather, with a satisfying clasp. We wandered the rooms and lifted trinkets from the tables. In the bathroom, I took so many soaps that my small purse exuded a dreamy lilac and honeysuckle smell.

Then, we were on the landing. Suddenly, everything was still. I crouched down and peered through the window, the square kind at the top of the stairs. They were kissing, my distant cousin and his distant bride, and the crowd assembled on the patio leaped to their feet and clapped and cheered.

"We missed it," my cousin sighed. "Now they're different forever."

What was it about the kiss that did this? Thinking of my mother's lip prints on envelopes, her cursive annotation—*SWAK!*

"I always close letters to your father like that." She pointed to the row of capitals. "It's an acronym. It means *sealed with a kiss.*"

"How are they different?" I wanted to know. "They look just the same as before."

My cousin lifted a votive candle from the window ledge, slipped it into her pocket. "Haven't you read your storybooks? The right kiss at the right time is the only way to break a spell."

old.

Jump rope chant: *First comes love, then comes marriage, then comes the baby in the baby carriage.*

I could see there was a proper sequence to things. It was like math, the way you had to add before you could multiply, then multiply before you could divide.

These were the words, three words like the peaks of three snowy mountains—*Love, Marriage, Baby.* You had to hike a long way, but mountain climbers had a word for this, too. They might plant a flag or drink a thermos of cocoa when they reached *the summit.* But what did you call the space between those summits?

"Do you mean the lowland?" my father asked. "The opposite of a mountain is a valley."

I could picture the valleys, too—snowy, deep, untrodden. It seemed every mountain had one. The valley beside Love was *Lonely.* The valley beside Marriage was *Single.* The valley beside Baby was *Childless.* How I wanted to find the crocus heads pushing up through that cold, cup them with my woolly mittens. How I wanted to lay myself down and make snow angels, one after the next until a path could be forged across the angels' bodies. Maybe then—it required a deep breath—maybe then those angels would bless the valleys where only the very sad or very brave dared to tread.

borrowed.

I had some confusion, though, about happily ever after. Did Prince Charming ever actually marry anyone? Could the Ash Girl or the Sleeping Beauty live happily ever after without a ring, without a dress, without whispering *I do*? Or a suite at the Marriott, for that matter? Or a baby that came the next year?

"Someday," my mother wept, "your father will give you away."

Newly skeptical, I heard myself say: "I think I would rather stay."

You see, I was beginning to understand about stories—how you could read them for the sounds they made, the pictures they painted in your mind. But then, when you went back to them, you could read again for something different. You could wriggle on your belly and sift through the soil until you found their meanings, which were hard little stones in your hands.

Everything Cinderella wore was borrowed, including the glass shoe. I felt uneasy about it—all that false pretense surrounding her one late night at the ball.

My father read to me for the last time from the big book of Disney favorites, read to me until I stopped him.

"But she was lying to the prince," I said. "Everyone says you're supposed to be yourself, but Cinderella came as someone else."

He shook his head. "No. She just wanted to put her best foot forward. She just wanted to look her best."

I rubbed one pebble around and around in my palm until it formed a tiny blister. "And what about that shoe? Why didn't it vanish with the rest of her things? By rights, he never should have been able to find her."

My father removed his glasses and wiped them with his handkerchief. "The way you're talking, it sounds like you wish he hadn't."

What of that? What if he hadn't? Could I change the story? Did I have that power?

The prince seemed like a dubious man. He claimed to love her, but he couldn't recognize her face? He needed the shoe to prove she was the one he had pledged his heart to?

"He even says it himself in the film. 'Do I love you because you're beautiful, or are you beautiful because I love you?' I think she's too good for him. I think the prince is a little bit shallow."

Now my father wrinkled his brow. His hands were clean and soft with no dirt beneath the nails. "I think you're reading too much into this," he said.

blue.

In the church pew, we find our offering envelopes, little wooden pencils to fill in the lines. Before she can stop me, I take my mother's blue ballpoint; I tithe my dime. Then, I check the box beside *Ms.* and print *Wade.*

"This one," my mother corrects, pointing to *Miss*. "It lets people know you're not married."

"I'm ten years old. I think they know."

"Still," she says, crossing it out. "You want to get into the habit."

old.

I study my parents' wedding album. Everything is white, including the cover, though it is stenciled with silver bells. Even the edges of the photographs are white, so you could write something if you wanted to, but no one has.

"The train of your dress is so long," I say. "Didn't you worry you would trip?"

"No. It's easier to walk than you would think, and I had my sister, the maid of honor, to smooth out the wrinkles and set everything straight."

"Did you like having so many people staring at you? I think I would blush or faint or something."

"When it happens, everything will be perfect, and you won't mind them looking. You'll be glad. You'll be giving hope to every young girl and single woman in the audience. Yours will be, for all those assembled, the face of love."

For some reason, at twelve, I turn easily queasy; I can't take comfort in the old truths anymore. Watching *The Sound of Music* with my mother, I walk out during Liesl's dance in the gazebo. This seems the best time to blow my nose, to forage for something to make a sandwich. When I return, she has paused it for me—Liesl in midair as Rolf spins her around, Cinderella-style. Her shoes, too, seem impractical.

"He's going to be a Nazi," I say.

"We don't know that yet," she replies.

But the scene where Fräulein Maria gets married is hard not to watch. It is hard to feign indifference to that grandeur. The music swells, the people rise, and my nose burns with tears I refuse to cry.

"This film came out two years before I married your father." My mother turns sentimental now, clipping her coupons and sipping her tea. "I kept going back to the theater for this—one scene in nearly three hours of screen time. I wanted to copy everything, right down to her crown of roses."

Fräulein Maria, who is also Julie Andrews, who is also my namesake and a woman whose beauty doesn't end with her face, fills me with inexplicable dread. From nun and nanny to wife and mother, I know I can't walk in her shoes. I haven't the patience for it—or the stamina. What's more: her shoes come secondhand from a man who must reject another woman, and before that, whose first wife had to die.

"Well, you can't marry someone when you're in love with someone else, can you?" Captain von Trapp asks Fräulein Maria when she questions him about the Baroness. He has the power to change the future, for not one but two women's lives.

blue.

We begin watching *Dr. Quinn, Medicine Woman* on Saturday nights as a family. It is "wholesome," my father lauds. "And Sully's so handsome," my mother beams.

Jane Seymour has one blue eye and one green, which is enough for me. My biology teacher calls this condition *heterochromia iridis*, which can be genetic or acquired. My history teacher reports that Jane Seymour was the third wife of Henry VIII, possibly his one true love. She is remembered for birthing Henry his only male heir, even as she died from complications after.

Dr. Quinn, who comes to the valley at the base of a mountain called Pikes Peak, is without love, marriage, or children. We learn her first name is Michaela, mistaken on a telegram for *Michael A*. No one expects a woman doctor. We learn she is thirty-five and has never been married, which requires an explanation. Her one true love—her betrothed—died in the Civil War. Now we can feel pity for her and not suspicion. She was trying to be a wife but was prevented by circumstances beyond her control.

We also learn that Dr. Quinn is a virgin, which is not the same as unmarried, but "should be," my father says. "It's nice to see a show with good, old-fashioned values for a change."

Even though I have studied the mechanics of sex in school, I find the prospect as remote as an island, as mythical as Atlantis. I am a virgin with two blue eyes and a little green of envy in my heart.

When Dr. Quinn marries Sully, who I understand is beautiful but for whom I must force a swoon, the crucial scene is the one that happens next. Will it be *happily*, this surrender of her virginity, this sequel to the wedding vow of wife? She has been alone in her body so long—twenty years longer than I. She has made a home in that valley, pitched her own tent, learned how to tend her own fire. Does Love have to lead to Marriage? Is this the only chairlift passing through the heart?

I take the VHS tape to my room in secret. I sit at the edge of the bed, my face close to the screen, scanning for shadows of uncertainty, resistance. Sully has made their marriage bed inside a train compartment. Her dress swaddles her into something half-child, half-swan. They seal again with a kiss, then draw the shades together. When he lays her down on the bed, she cups the back of his head, consenting. He contains the music, I understand then; she waits for the dancing to begin.

borrowed.

"I'm a little concerned," the teacher at my Catholic high school says. "I asked you to write about a ritual in your faith. I don't see how what transpires here is a ritual."

"It's a wedding," I tell her. "Aren't weddings a ritual in any faith?"

"Yes, but—" I have been summoned to her office. This is not the first time. She thinks I am troubled but also promising. Ambivalence hangs in the air between us. "You realize this isn't really about the wedding."

"Is it ever?" I have been practicing my enigmatic face, shortening my sentences for effect.

"I think perhaps you've misunderstood the purpose of this assignment. In describing the ritual, I wanted you to consider its significance."

"I have. The wedding exists to prove a marriage has taken place, and the marriage exists so the man can take the woman."

The teacher is married, which means she has been taken, though she has not taken her husband's name. *Ms.* A married woman who is not a *Mrs.*

"I need to confirm—" she uncaps her pen as if she is going to make a mark of some kind—"I need to confirm this didn't really happen to you."

"I've never been married," I shrug.

"Not the marriage—the *rape*." The word is so hot I think it must burn the roof of her mouth to say it.

"What rape? This is a story about a girl who marries her high school sweetheart."

"No. This is a story about a young woman who marries the only man she has ever known, and then he takes her to her childhood home and ties her hands to the wicker headboard and—*has his way with her.*" Thank goodness for euphemisms. She never would have made it through that sentence without them.

"It's a metaphor," I say calmly, almost mechanically. "It's about a loss of innocence. That's why I put baby's breath on her windowsill and dolls on the bed that he has to sweep aside."

"But it's not true?" she makes me promise, holding my eyes a long time.

"Not *literally*, no," though I do have a wicker headboard.

"So why did you write it?" She lets her pen trace the length of my margin.

"I wanted to look at a different ritual besides the wedding itself—the one no one talks about but everyone implies."

"Consummation," she nods.

"To me, even though I've never been consummated"—I feel the need to reassure her now—"it seems like the place where *borrowed* meets *appropriation.*"

"Can you say a little more about that?" Her brows have come together in a dark line; her lips, which are thin and pale, pucker with concern.

"No. I really don't think I can."

new.

In the Sharon Olds poems I read in college, sex is a new, rare, coveted thing. The way she writes it makes me want to want it, makes me wonder if I ever will. Then, I remember—like a dream that returns all day, bit by bit, in fragments—that I *do* want it, that I *have.* Only where was sex in the old sequence? Could it come before Love? Must it come after Marriage? (It was only clear that sex must precede Baby in the baby carriage.)

At the central desk in the Mormon genealogy room in Salt Lake City: "Are you married yet?" the woman sweetly inquires.

"Me?"

She nods and smiles.

"I'm—I'm only nineteen," I stammer.

"It's never too early to start your family planning." A pamphlet with a husband and wife and many rosy children—everyone white and clad in khaki—appears beside me on the counter. I never see her hand. She seems to move the pamphlet with her mind.

"That's OK," I say. "I already have a plan."

In my dorm closet, I assess the stash. One jug of Carlo Rossi wine, the only kind I could find in the pantry at home. This will help to put us in the mood, to soothe our nerves—should there ever be an us and a reason to be nervous. Also, many condoms from Campus Health, pilfered from a small woven basket when the receptionist stepped out to heat her lunch. I don't know how many I will need, so I take all of them. I only know there must not be a baby in a baby carriage.

Finally, a pack of cigarettes. Marlboro Reds—because I once heard a tattooed barista tell a suave-seeming man that they were sexy. Also, a book of matches. People seem to want cigarettes after. I've seen all the movies, some of them several times. At least in bed then, after the sweat and the swoon, when words become insufficient, I won't have to wonder what comes next. I'll have something to do with my mouth and my hands.

borrowed.

Home from college now, restless in my parents' church. The weddings and baptisms have all been announced. The preacher has read from the big book of laws and parables. I slip five dollars into the envelope, which feels less like a gift than a bribe.

My mother watches as my hand hovers above *Ms.* "What did I tell you about that designation?"

Recently, I have become irate about double standards. Everything is grounds for comparison. "Look," I whisper. "Men are always *Mr.* their whole lives. They never have to change their prefix, and no one expects them to change their names. I won't do it either. It isn't fair."

"So, you're going to be that kind of woman then? You've made up your mind?" She signs her check in flourished script—the first name hers, the last name borrowed.

Anger opens inside me like a rose. I take her pen and check the box beside *Mr.*

blue.

In a poem she wrote to her daughter, Sharon Olds makes the following prediction: "That night will come. Somewhere someone will be entering you, his body riding under your white body, dividing your blood from your skin . . . "

Only for you, it is day, and the sky is rippling blue in that soft, September way; only faint wisps of cloud annotate its margins. It is also your birthday, and you have given yourself this gift, which in another light is also a bribe.

Later, you arrive at your parents' house to play the good daughter again, the one who saves herself for marriage, the one who faithfully abstains.

But the sequence and the startled opening and the feeling like the flutter of trapped birds and then the glimpse of something as through a skylight returns to you in dream-haze all day.

You are not ashamed the way your mother promised you would be. This is the first surprise. But it is not like the poems promised either. You do not feel a great cathedral inside. Instead, like someone opened an umbrella indoors, and you are the indoors, he the umbrella with the sharp points and the too-wide smile.

Perhaps—an unsettling thought—*you are not a Modern Woman after all.* Your mother passes the piping hot rolls. Your father mentions the weather: how mild it has been, how serene. But isn't he the same person who always said "It's calmest before the storm"?

It might be in fact—an intriguing thought—*that you are a Postmodern Woman.* You are the one who comes after, who does not play by her mother's rules, but neither does she play by their converse. Less chart and graph, less dotted line. More dark mosaic and white noise.

new.

It is long in coming, but we know it, the way we always know. My best friend's wedding, like the arrival of a train, people on the platform remarking, "Why, lookie there. Right on time."

"Will you stand with me at the altar?" she asks. "Will you read a sonnet for us in blessing?"

Will she be erased by him, her gentle husband? Will he be erased by her?

So I stand and read. I play the part of witness—the part I know so well—the part I know best of all. It is important not to seem jealous. (*Am I?*) It is important not to begrudge. (*Do I?*)

There are calla lilies on my dress, the dress I have chosen. Later, a woman tells me they are the flower of death. "Don't worry, dear. You didn't know."

A furtive look on my face, a blush cresting my cheeks. Ambivalence hangs in the air between us.

new.

This is the last time my parents will dance together, or this is the last time I will see them dance, so it is final for me: the way a photograph preserves its subject exactly as she was and cannot account for changes to follow.

There they are, my parents, as vivid in memory as they are that day in the chilly church basement, gliding across the checkered floor, swaying in time to the big band tunes. And perhaps I'm feeling a little wistful now, watching them from a folding chair with a Styrofoam cup in my hand—wistful that I will not be—that indeed, for me, there is no way to be—a blushing bride, a Mrs. So-and-So, the emulation they have always longed for.

"Do you feel sad?" my mother asks when she pauses for a cookie and some punch.

"Sad? No. Why should I be sad?"

"Well, it's hard, I know, being surrounded by so many couples. But your time will come, and we'll all dance on your wedding day."

"Mom—"

"Yes?" She is powdering her shiny skin into a plain matte finish.

"Why are we here again?"

"Well, Nancy's my friend, and she and her husband wanted to renew their vows."

"But they're vows. Aren't they supposed to last forever?"

"Of course they are, but it's just that her family's been through so much, and they've weathered it all—every last storm. Now don't stare, but—" She makes a subtle gesture toward a young woman in a tight black dress. I had noticed her earlier: the freckled arms and cropped red hair, the body that seemed afraid to ever stop moving. "That's Nancy's daughter, and in the last two years, she has dropped over a hundred pounds."

"Oh." I am not sure what to say. (*Is there a right thing to say?*)

"On the road to spinsterhood," my mother gleams, "someone just made a U-turn!" Then, she swivels her gaze toward a young man, dark and stalwart, standing beside the pass-through window. "And Nancy's son—see him there? He used to be gay, and now he's not anymore. I hear he's even found himself a girlfriend."

Many thoughts still require images to explain them, especially in the absence of certain words. No one will tell you that there is a place apart from the mountain and the valley, separate from the summit and the lowland. Sometimes it is concealed by a waterfall, which everyone recognizes as a symbol of passion. For example, many lovers stand at Snoqualmie Falls and kiss each other fervently; some even recite their vows and exchange their rings against the roar of water cresting over the rocks.

This is the dangerous side of Love. They like it, even though they are afraid.

But below and behind that glistening spume, I can picture it now— what Thomas Wolfe had called "an unfound door." If you open it, you can step through the mountain and change your trajectory entirely. No longer ascending or descending, you can traverse the landscape of the underside, the unspoken. I have approached that keyhole many times in my mind, but it too is dangerous, and I am still afraid to peer inside.

My father extends his hand to me, and I startle. "Sweetheart," he says, "may I have this dance?"

new.

The new millennium makes me want to do something extraordinary and daring—maybe even mountain-climb. I work with a man who makes me laugh sometimes, who shows me the way the shoes lie flat in their box: "Like opening a quote, then adding an apostrophe." He smiles his best, syntactic smile. We work on commission, the way everyone does, whether they know it or not.

Once, in an elevator with him, I pressed the STOP button. I meant the opposite. I meant READY, SET, GO. I wanted so much to be like those women in the movies, leaning in and leaning back, playing coy and enjoying it. Beneath my starched white collar and my pinstriped skirt, I could feel myself tremble, tipping: a barrel poised on a waterfall.

It would have been fitting if the Muzak had played, "No one knows what goes on behind closed doors," Charlie Rich soulfully crooning. I did, in fact, let my hair hang down, and he was glad then to be a certain kind of man.

When the doors opened, though, I should have been a certain kind of woman: palms slick with concupiscence, heart in her throat like a wild bird. Instead, I smoothed my skirt and walked toward the break room calmly. I can still hear my solid heels clicking on the newly shined floor.

blue.

For our wedding, we agree to meet in the orchard. It is our long ago and far away, our fairy-tale landscape after all. His brother is a priest, and I have two friends to act as witnesses. What I want is small and simple and private: a dress without a train and a blue car waiting in the underbrush.

"I'll rent a convertible," he promises. "We'll drive all day to the beach."

One friend is married; she encourages me. "This is where it leads," she says. "Not an end at all—a new beginning." I can tell from one hour in their home that she loves her husband as I have never loved my fiancé.

My other friend is single and silent on matters such as these. As I stand before the three-way mirror, I ask her to fasten the clasp, secure the zipper. "I never wear dresses anymore," I blush. The hot lights of the fitting room, her hand on my back like a flame. I am marked now, in a way I cannot erase.

"What about the bouquet? Will you have one?"

"Irises," I say. "A bundle of them, almost in disarray. So blue they are almost purple."

Something—it is not ambivalence—hangs in the air between us.

new.

Instead. This is the word on the little gold plaque on the large wood door beneath the waterfall. You can knock as long as you want, but no one will answer. Your voice will ricochet and return to you in that cavern, and you may feel, for a moment, more alone than you ever have.

It is worth noting that your parents have also receded into the past. They are smaller now, in retrospect—like the wax figures atop a wedding cake, joined at the arm but gazing away from each other, not toward. The deep spell of their long governance has been broken.

Instead. In lieu of. Otherwise.

Look for the key in your pocket. If you don't have a pocket, you might need to change your clothes.

borrowed.

Carole Maso writes, "We're a little lost. In the semiotics. And not a graduate student in sight."

We are the graduate students. We are a little lost. Not even the semiotics can save us.

We pass our days in communal space and spend our nights in rented rooms, and we are furtive and foolish and unable to stop what we have started. We hock the man's wedding band and go for Thai food. We travel around, my wedding dress in the trunk of her car, like a library book long overdue. (*Think of the stories it couldn't tell.*) Paper airplanes are made from the marriage license.

Then, one morning, many years in the future, I wake, and my pockets have sprouted flowers. There they are, fresh as clover in the neighbor's lawn. I lie still a long time, struggling to believe they are mine.

blue.

It is time. Another friend has summited the mountain and strolled the scenic bridge—from Love to its adjacent peak. (*Is Wedding the signifier? Is Marriage the signified?*)

She asks me to read for her, to walk ahead of her in a satin dress and stand at the altar in her honor. (*In her shadow?*) My love sits alone in the crowd; someone rolls a carpet down the makeshift aisle. Years have passed. We are happy after everything. (Her eyes, cerulean, squinting in the sudden sun.) Years have passed. We are happy for everything to come. (Her skirt and blouse, the real body I have glimpsed beneath them.) Peaceful in our paradox—not *Single*, not *Married* either. What are we? What is this—our *Something Else*?

I stand at the altar, she sits in her chair, and all at once the old rose of anger blooms in my throat, choking me as I try to recite—*"How shall we speak of love except in the splurge of roses, and the long body of the river shining in its silk froth"*?

Of course we tell the story of rose and river. These belong to everyone, to all lovers everywhere, united in romantic fancy. *But we are not only speaking of Love!* My nostrils flair as I consider it at last: the blue body paragraph, the red margin line, that vast topography of difference. It is not the rose and river only, but the wedding rite, the honeymoon, the married life that follows. That familiar algorithm (part math, part witchcraft): Love converts to Marriage after a spell. *SWAK!* But it doesn't—it hasn't—not for us.

Later, my love says, "Yes, you have lost something. It was not something you were sure you wanted, but you have lost it nonetheless."

Not the ring! Not the dress!

Instead: "It was the *choice*—to choose or not to choose. What you lost was the *possibility of.*"

For the moment, then: too much champagne like a drum in my head, the catapult of the loose bouquet.

"I'm next!" a triumphant voice exclaims.

The tears on my cheeks, slowly singeing: *I'm not! Not once. Not ever again.*

new.

"I welcome your anger," the therapist says. "I want you to speak in an uncensored way—whatever you need to say."

"I'm suspicious of therapy."

He laughs as he reaches for his steno pad; I notice his thin, gold band.

"I'm suspicious of marriage, too—almost as much as therapy."

He nods as he jots something down. "But suspicion is different from contempt, isn't it?"

Cautiously now: "What do you mean?"

"Well, we aren't only suspicious of things we disclaim. Often, we're suspicious of things we desire. Sometimes, even, of things we're afraid to desire."

I fold my arms across my chest the way my students do—posture of recalcitrance, resistance. "So, you're saying you think I want to get married? That it scares me because I do?"

"Does it? Do you?"

"It's not that simple." I'm flustered and faintly embarrassed, too. "Maybe it isn't even about marriage exactly." *Is Marriage only the subject? Is Something Else the theme?*

"No?" He meets my eyes, holds them until I look away—back to his hand, back to his ring. The thing that divides us. *Or does it?*

"I'm usually so much more articulate than this," I sigh. "I just—it's about entitlement. That's the theme. That's my objection to marriage."

"So if everyone could freely choose marriage, if it were an equal right, you'd be married? You and your partner would walk down to the courthouse and sign the contract today?"

I want to say it is so. I wait for the word—*true, indeed, affirmative*—like a bell set to ring at a certain time. Instead, *Yes* is melting on my tongue; then, *No* is melting on my tongue. They are the snow, and I am the warm ground, the warm sound of *Maybe*.

"Maybe," I say.

"Can you say a little more about that?" His face is calm and kind; his pen traces a dotted line across the page.

I study his ring and shake my head. "No. I really don't think I can."

old.

There are two women we know, friends, we are lucky to call them. They have been "together forever," they say. A decade at least—which sounds like forever to us.

By all accounts, they have a good life. Since Pennsylvania is not a marriage state, they have what many would call "domestic partnership."

Some romance is lost in that phrase, yet marriage still implies a husband and wife. The one is businesslike, the other rife with hints of old dominion.

An invitation comes in the mail, cardstock square of plain black script: "Please join us for our wedding celebration."

It is Pittsburgh. It is August in the park. Coneflowers and goldenrod and the purple haze of summer that hangs in the air between us. They grin and wave, the bride and bride in slacks and shirts and bright Hawaiian leis. They say, "We figured, why not bring the beach to us?"

There are these familiar things—the speaking of vows, the giving of rings—but no frazzled family, no store-bought bouquets. No minister officiates, no photographer directs. Neither woman's father walks her down the aisle. Their names, paratactic on the page, remain unchanged.

We stand and smile among the witnesses, our glasses clinking through the singing, the dancing, and the stories told. We toast to their long love, to their enduring happiness. Several times, I find warm water seeping from my eyes.

"Do you feel different?" I ask my friend.

"I'm sure I will," she quips, "when the bill comes."

"No, I mean—does the ceremony change things between you? Do you think it will?"

"It isn't change so much as consecration."

This word now, instead of consummation, instead of the old edicts against "living in sin." But how was this a new way of living in love?

"What about the laws?" I press.

The platinum band swivels on her finger. "What about them?"

If a wedding doesn't mark a marriage . . . *I'm a little lost in the semiotics . . .* what is it a marker for?

blue.

I'm sad, and I don't know how to express it. I resent them—all the married people I have ever known, but I envy them, too, and, if I'm honest, feel a bit smug, a bit . . . *superior.*

Every day my Love walks the tightrope without a net. Every day they have the whole circus to support them. Think how brave my Love is, by comparison.

"So, let me understand," he says. "You don't want to marry your partner, but you believe you should have the *right* to marry her if you choose?"

"The first part is sometimes true; the second part is always true."

"But you also wish that no one else would marry? That there would be a moratorium on marriage?"

"Just until the laws change. Just until everyone is equal."

"And has it been your experience," he asks, "that legislation results in equality?" His gray eyes narrow and focus; he wants to get it right. "Do you believe that laws change people's minds?"

"Not all at once, not overnight, but—" I grow sweaty in my uncertainty; the tears redirect to my palms.

"Let me ask you this: Suppose everyone stopped marrying until everyone could marry, and then suppose you and everyone else married the person that each of you loved. You were all spouses; you were all equal before the law. What happens then? Does it all go on, happily ever after?"

"Why not? Why *shouldn't* it if it always has?" That rose in my belly, my throat, blossoming now in its dark splendor. "I gave a ring to my partner years ago! I profess my love for her every day! If we were a common couple under common law, we'd be married. Wedding or not," I repeat it for emphasis, "we'd be married."

"And would you be happy," his pen strikes the page, "being just another common couple under the common law?"

old.

A poem on my pillow, a poem to sleep on:

I think I grow tensions
like flowers
in a wood where
nobody goes.

Each wound is perfect,
encloses itself in a tiny
imperceptible blossom,
making pain.

Pain is a flower like that one,
like this one,
like that one,
like this one.

blue.

In a dream, I return to the orchard where I once loved a man—my best attempt of those long years of Almost, Not Quite. I stand in the high grass under the apple tree and remember the picnics, remember our clothes cast off after the picnics, our bodies becoming Something Else.

Then, I stand at the turn of the road and remember my absence, that old elopement I managed to elope from. *How had I come to say that I would come? How had I made this promise to him—as if our lives were only a catalog page, mine to cut and alter?*

In the dream, I do not wear the white dress. I do not carry the velvet box with the man's thick band inside. My love holds long-stemmed irises in her lovely hands, blue as twilight and so many she can barely grasp them. We wear blue jeans and canvas shoes. We are not expecting a special occasion.

"Look into my eyes," she says. They are blue also, like the sea or the sky. "Not these irises," shaking the flowers as she shakes her head. They make a gentle, rustling sound. "*These*."

I glimpse the ticker at the dark corner of the dream: *Your life with her—that is the special occasion.*

new.

I want to say, like Chagall, "Only love interests me," but Love is not the story. A new thought, nearly an epiphany. Love is the canvas, the texture of the page, the ink in the pen or the paint on the brush. I spend hours gazing at his paintings. They are not Love—they are Something Else—but Love is the raw material.

This is what interests me—montage, stream of consciousness, the flow and shift of words, the flux of moments glimpsed as if through a kaleidoscope. Scenes without narratives to connect them. Some notion of an essence.

I have always wanted to belong without being claimed. To be a wife would mean I am wanted, but it would not confirm, and in fact might obscure, the truth of what *I* want. Often, I have felt that I could not bear it—this cultural imperative—yet it is hard to look away from the chosen ones, to surrender envy and even admiration.

Have I spurned marriage because I feared I would never be chosen?

My best friend, whom I will lose in the aftermath, the way numbers in a problem are sometimes left over and will not resolve—I become her vexing remainder.

"I'm really surprised by your casualness." The words singe as she speaks them. "You claim you love this woman, but you won't even have a commitment ceremony?"

"Our love is between us!"

"But your commitment should be made before God and everyone."

Have I spurned marriage to make a point, to defy her judgment and win this argument?

The sign on my professor's door: "The real question is not whether the state should marry queers but whether the state should marry anyone."

So why do I resent a civil union? Why does it feel "less than," if marriage is only more of what I don't trust and don't need?

"You know I love you," another friend says, standing at the counter beside a steeping cup of tea. "But remember, being part of a couple carries privileges, too. I know, being single all these years, how I am looked down upon. *No one wanted her,* they think. *She must be afraid to make a commitment. So immature!*" The steam rising. "*Who can we set her up with? It's such a shame to think of her alone.*" The steam continuing to rise. "*If only she had some-one—that would really put my mind at ease.*

"I'm not saying everyone recognizes you as a couple, or if they do, that they see your partnership as equivalent to marriage." She is discerning and searches for the right word: "as *equally valid* as a marriage. But, how much of your desire to be recognized as partnered is about not wanting to be con-fused with someone like me—about not wanting to be presumed *single*?"

"But I'm *not* single," I murmur.

"Exactly. You're not single—whether anyone thinks you are or not."

On the medical form:
(check one) Single   Married   Separated   Divorced   Widowed

"Do you have any family I should call?" the surgeon asks before the anes-thesia takes hold.

"I have family. She's sitting in the waiting room." Now my heart begins to thump—earnestly, defensively.

On the medical form:
(check one) Single   Married   Separated   Divorced   Widowed

"Oh, I'm sorry," he replies, his wedding band visible beneath his latex gloves. *I can't help but look, can't help but wonder . . .* "My nurse mentioned you were unmarried."

On the medical form:
(check one) Single   Married   Separated   Divorced   Widowed

When I wake, still groggy in the hospital bed: "I know what I would say— my vow."

"Do you?"

"I'm not saying we should have a wedding. I'm not saying we need a wedding. But—" She looks so beautiful in the morning light, with her glasses on and a book in her hand.

Fading out again, I whisper. "It's Eliot. He knew. _We are the music while the music lasts._"

old.

It has been ten years now. Do we qualify as "together forever"?

During our decade of undocumented love, six states and one district have legalized same-sex marriage. During our decade of unnotarized affection, twelve states have prohibited same-sex marriage via statute, another twenty-nine via state constitution. On paper, it looks like we are losing. On paper, there is a push toward our erasure.

How can marriage be both the Pink Pearl of erasure and the Pink Pearl that prevents our erasure?

"Wild idea," I propose over breakfast. "Since we've always had a Boston marriage, why don't we go ahead and have a Boston marriage?"

"Maybe, if we lived in Boston, that would make sense. I don't see how that serves us here in the Bluegrass State."

"It depends," I say. "It doesn't make sense if we think of the marriage as purely practical—a legal document. But it does make sense if we think of the marriage as Something Else—as something symbolic."

"I don't think of marriage that way," she replies.

"Oh."

Softening: "Do you?"

The snow and the warm ground again: "Maybe."

She is quiet in her certainty, as she has always been. "To me, there doesn't seem any point in marrying unless we gain the same legal benefits as everyone who is married. What else will a marriage give us that we don't already have?"

I know the answer. I think I have always known. _Disappointment, relief—what is the precise word for this feeling?_ "Nothing," I say, after a time.

"But you're sad—I can tell. Why?"

"Not sad. It isn't sad exactly." I think of the immense waterfall and the swollen wood door, one whole world waiting on the underside and one whole world left behind. "I'm just a little _crestfallen_," I finally confide.

I have been known to do this, too—to grow a forest and hide behind the thickest trunks of the hardest words, to stand in their tall, semantic shadows. It is as if by naming a feeling, I will find a way to contain it. As if the feeling itself will submit beneath the cunning blade of my tongue.

Then, she kisses me, and a new spell is made and broken.

blue.

In a dream, we are standing on the seashore, our pant legs cuffed and our fingers laced. As we walk together toward the gathering fog, small waves lap at our feet.

This is the perfect setting for a wedding, I realize.

I turn to her, and she points to a piece of driftwood farther up the beach. Tied to the log is the largest bouquet of balloons I have ever seen. Each one is a different shade of blue.

"What are these for?" I ask. "Is it some kind of celebration?"

She doesn't answer. Instead, she kneels in the cool sand and begins to untie them. The many white strings are knotted, tethered to the log but also tangled with each other. I watch as she works diligently to release each balloon from the bunch.

They are Love, they are Marriage, they are Children. They are also their concomitants, the highlighted and the implied: Sex, Wedding, Fertility. The blue balloons are a collection of certainties, of wishes and fears and secret anticipations. In my dreams, I know nothing but understand all.

One by one, we let the balloons go, separate from us and separate from each other. We are wistful, we are joyful, we are silent in our task. We stand a long time in the morning light, watching, then forgetting to watch.

Tremolo

That I have studied love through male lenses occurs to me now. *Agape*, the unconditional love of God for man, is the story of a son who did not fail his father—unlike the rest of us, selfish and unholy. Even *Eros*, the lesser love of humankind, is represented by a chubby, mischievous boy. Valentine's Day—though the province of lovers, though the holiday when manifestations of Eros are most likely to appear—celebrates man's love for woman, where love suggests passion, romance, and sexual desire.

The woman's story, I fear, has been occluded in this history of quest and conquer. Does she have dialogue? Will she initiate an act of longing? How will she know, recognize, and respond to love? Or is she always, at best, an adjudicator, evaluating the performance of men, the chivalry and championship of suitors, stumbling over each other in their rush to woo?

When I was nineteen, a diligent college student—obsessed with abstraction, flirtatious with philosophy—I dissected love fiercely, squinted at it from every angle, toed the lip of the tub that might contain love, unsure or unwilling to descend. By this time, I had read Dickinson, Whitman, and Frost, dubbed them "lyric philosophers" in lieu of "poets," poetry seeming to me then too flimsy a term for such measured and meritorious contemplation. Of course, all the poets were dead, and all the philosophers, too— Kant and Mill, Russell and Rousseau—which left me wondering whether love would be given over to science for good. Oxytocin elation. Sympathetic and parasympathetic response. "Fight or flight"—which was just a fancy way of saying "love 'em or leave 'em."

Kirsten, who was my roommate and also my friend, cautioned against this growing reliance on science. "Everything you need to know about love is available through your own English major. Who do you like to read?"

"The Brontës, Austen some, Defoe, Swift . . . "

"Anything American? Anything from the here and now?"

I shrugged and gazed at my bookshelf, which was crowded with gilded texts that came as a set for Christmas. The look of these books had been more important at the time than their contents. "Usually, I read whatever's put in front of me. Or I go to the library and pick something off the shelf at random."

Kirsten's brow bent, her bright eyes clouded. "I think people write love poems for a reason," she said as she scanned the symmetrical tumult of her own shelves. "They aren't guidebooks. They don't come with instructions. But"—she reached for a slender white volume—"consider this a travelogue from a place everyone wants to visit."

I took the book in my hands like the penitent I was, receiving my first communion. "My favorites," she said, "are 'The Night' and 'Rapture.' I think I'd like a portion of each read at my wedding."

That was another thing: Kirsten wasn't merely an expert on love-texts; she had conducted her own field research. Nathan, the man she loved, was her one and only. They met when she was seventeen in a Running Start community college class. He painted houses and took photographs. He was older slightly, and calmer, with extraordinary eyes. Now she wore his ring on the fourth finger of her left hand—a small but unmistakable diamond. And this meant that she was promised, that love existed for her apart from and beyond its abstraction, like a creature crawled out of its shell.

~

Eight years later, I think of that book again. I am living my own love story now but marveling at how I arrived.

Angie and I reside in Ohio, which my West Coast imagination could barely conjure before. What was this state but a placemat promise shaded gray or gold? An impossible place—yet I have loved and been loved here beyond abstraction.

The Barnesville Public Library has everything by Dickinson, Whitman, and Frost. The shelves are packed tight and precise with posthumous heroes, lyric philosophers. "I'm looking for a poet," I say. "Galway Kinnell."

"Never heard of him," the woman behind the desk replies. "*Him*?"

I nod.

She shifts her weight and considers my face, then shakes the mouse beneath her mottled hand. "And the book you're looking for?"

"That's the trouble," I reply. "It's been a long time. I can't quite recall . . . I was hoping I'd know it when I saw it."

~

Some nights Kirsten would read to me with the fortitude of a woman recit-
ing her rosary. She knew the words in such a way that she did not require
the page. Her effortless turning and her wandering eyes gave her quickly
away.

I remember best the image of a man holding a woman from behind.
They had just made love, a ritual so rife with passion and pleasure I could
not believe it existed at all. Yet, in this blissful state, this epilogue, he held
her: her small body propped against his larger; his large body propped
against the pillows or the wall, with morning light seeping in through the
blinds. And he was described as *the big, folded wings of her*, words I never
forgot but turned over and over inside my mind, rotisserie of wonder and
surprise.

The woman was an angel, of course. And the man a kind of angel too,
watching over.

But some nights Kirsten didn't stay in the room. She packed her pillow
and an overnight bag—or *portmanteau,* as she was fond of saying. We were
both writers. We hearkened to the thrill of words, particularly those that
were strange or out-of-date. Antiquation could only increase their value, we
reasoned.

When she went to Nathan's room, we never spoke about her destination, what acts of literature they might emulate beneath the dormitory
sheets. She was gone, and I lay awake in my bunk with a book-light, envy-
ing the women of those poems, their luxury of being seen so completely,
their power to incite such desire.

~

There was a boy then. We were mostly friends. But one night, I let the
moonlight get the better of me, the way a Brontë would, and I kissed him
suddenly on the balcony with kids playing hacky sack below. He left my
good red sweater wilted with palm-sweat. We didn't speak again for days.

Then, the night came. We had only half-planned it. I waited quietly for
Kirsten to leave. Lighting candles was a conduct violation, to say nothing
of sneaking in men. I wore satin pajamas. He asked me to cover my eyes
while he changed into his. Though bent on Mexico, we were both prepared
to turn back at El Paso.

"Here," I whispered, thrusting the book into his hand. "I've marked a
couple of pages. Kirsten doesn't mind. We could read aloud to each other."

This was sexy, right? This was what lovers did?

We crowded onto my bed side by side. As he read, the words began to lose their beauty. They came out forced and stilted, the awkward scene seeming to describe anything but love. I tried, blushing hard, to continue: "*Her moans come with a slight delay . . .* "

"I'm not sure I can do this," he said.

"We don't have to do anything much. You could just stay with me, hold me."

"Should we blow out the candles?"

"Yes."

"Should we take off our clothes?"

"Yes."

In the dark, we shivered together; his body small and sharp as a paring knife, mine soft and self-consciously larger. *Isn't he supposed to be bigger than me?* He was the man after all, yet he seemed to have no instinct for it. We did not fit together right. Clearly, we were doing something wrong. I thought of the poem: *Their bones almost hit—the purpose of flesh may be to keep the skeletons from bruising each other.* Yet there we were, bruised and rattled. I could feel his ribs spearing me, every sharp edge. As I listened to his shallow breath, I knew he was not sleeping either. We lay awake all night like toys in a box, longing to come apart.

If you had told me in college that I would someday love a woman, I would have told you solemnly and with a hint of regret that you had mistaken me for someone else. I was fated to be a failed heterosexual. I never intended to become a successful queer.

To our good fortune, we outgrow ourselves. Ohio proves a landscape we can envisage at last, beautiful in ways we never dreamed. My good fortune is doubled, though, for I, a lover of books, fell in love with a librarian.

The second poem "Rapture" is a poem about morning. Not any morning, mind you, but the fabled Morning After. Here the poet describes the pleasant voyeurism of watching his beloved dress to meet the day. But first—*I have been lying with eyes shut, thinking, or possibly dreaming, of how she might look if, at breakfast, I spoke about the hidden place in her which, to me, is like a soprano's tremolo.*

I did not know what a *tremolo* was, so I had to look it up—discretely, for I feared repercussions somehow. He was talking about a place inside her. Was he allowed to say this? It seemed scandalous, if also erotic; the two might not mutually exclude. We were walking around with this place inside of us, *women*, like a secret trousseau, something we could not experience ourselves except in poetic translation or breakfast conversation . . . the men who might open it, peruse its contents.

My first Morning After, following the night when next to nothing happened: he was gone, and my back ached, and I was grateful for my own bed again, all to myself in the errant light.

At breakfast, I saw him across the cafeteria, eating cereal alone, flipping through a paper. "Why don't you go and talk to him?" Kirsten nudged.

"Oh, no . . . he looks busy. I don't want to bother him."

"Even after last night?"

"It isn't what you think," I began to protest.

"But he did stay?"

"Yes."

"And now you're not speaking?"

"Not exactly . . . it's just hard to know what to say."

A tremolo, similar to vibrato, is a term in music for the repetition of the same note, rapidly, over and over. I think of it sometimes as a stutter—what I can't put into words but want to. Or as a history—where themes repeat themselves despite our best intentions to correct them, to make a clean break. How it was all foreshadowed: that I would be with men; that I would not feel about them as I thought I should—as the poems made me wish I could. That I would wonder if other women did, or if their love stories were also part pantomime, part bravado, a performance they had learned so well the best of them forgot they were acting at all.

~

"It's called *Imperfect Thirst*," Angie smiles.

"What is?"

"The book . . . : the book of poems by Galway Kinnell . . . containing 'The Night' and 'Rapture.' Those are the ones you said you wanted, right?"

"Yes." I sit up in bed. She has a laptop and a lovely spine. I listen to her fingers clicking on the keyboard, the reassuring sound of her research, which is merely music by another name.

"So I'll order it for you, and it'll come in a few days. We just have to pick it up in town." Then, turning around with a furtive look in her eyes: "What's this for? Why the urgency? Are you teaching these poems next term?"

"Not hardly. No, I—" tracing her long neck, the tantalizing line of her—"I just need to complete a recollection."

~

When Kirsten married Nathan, in the first summer of the new millennium, I read a poem for them. I did not read from "The Night" or "Rapture" but from something more suitable for her audience—"less intimate, more time-less," she said. And so, nervously, though I didn't need the small collection of Shakespeare's sonnets I clasped in my hand, I turned to 116 and spoke from my heart: "*Let me not to the marriage of true minds admit impediments. Love is not love which alters when it alteration finds . . .*"

But didn't love change us? Wasn't that why we were all so desperate for it, waving our flags in the wind, waiting for a ratty cloth of raw intention to become a sail that could take us somewhere?

In graduate school, I went on to study poetry. I came back again to Dickinson, Whitman, and Frost. Kinnell also was a question on my comprehensive exam. Rather, I should say, he proved an opportunity for consideration, one of several poets I might have written about, though he frightened me then with his narratives of natural love—one woman, one man, their desire for each another so inevitable, it seemed. I was afraid the story of his poem might someday be used against me.

~

Now the book has arrived, and I open it like boarding a plane back in time. I cannot wait to bring it home, so I sit in the car shivering, the heat coming on slowly, the engine straining against the cold. I return to the man thinking of the tremolo inside the woman's body, how he watches her dressing in the morning, leaning over her underwear drawer. I have watched this scene, and I have been this scene, where a man watches me from the bed. This is ordinary, I think. This is commonplace.

He describes *the two mounds of muscle* of her backside, effuses at their beauty. Why do I feel uneasy with his words? I, too, love my lover's body. I, too, have written poems that sing her praise. This man, this speaker, seems sincere, even if excessive. And doesn't love make us silly? Doesn't love lend itself readily to hyperbole?

Women too, women who sleep with men joyfully and deliberately, tell us of this desire to be admired. I have context for it now: a rolodex of references, footnotes falling like confetti on New Year's Day. Sandra Cisneros writes, *You're in love with my mind. But sometimes, sweetheart, a woman needs a man who loves her ass.* And this is what the woman in Kinnell's poem needs also—not just *wants* but *needs.* Whether the need is innate or imitative, instinctive or learned, who can say? We know only that the speaker's lover immediately returns to bed and begins unbuttoning his pajamas. He initiates, however, by first reaching out for her, touching her hand. His admiration kindles her desire, and her desire reignites his admiration. This is the circle their story forms.

I'm still uneasy, overheating in a parked car, thinking of the lover's need to gaze upon the beloved. I wonder: *When is this love, and when is it voyeurism?*

When we stop really seeing the other person? When the imposition of our own longing distorts and overwhelms her presence?

At the end of the poem, the man speaks for the woman with great authority, as if his knowledge of her body has granted safe passage through the portal of her mind—as if knowing one part of her entitles him to speak for all of her: *she will be, all day among strangers, looking down inside herself at our rapture.* Is it self-congratulatory? Does this conclusion suggest a sub-genre of love poems I have learned to recognize and avoid? (I-made-her-come-and-now-she's-grateful poems?)

I tuck the book under the seat with the atlas and the ice-scrapers. I drive the short distance home.

~

It's true I was always troubled by love: romantic love, unrequited love, the cult of finding The One and keeping him. Was love that easy to lose?

The women I knew were mostly unhappy in marriage, yet they pitied the women who were without men. To be unmarried, let alone divorced, was to be marked by the world as a creature of sorrow, of great misfortune. Yet *having* a man, holding the coveted title of *wife*, seemed only to generate aggravation. It was a socially sanctioned aggravation at that, and women spent their time together despairing of their husbands' stupidity and selfishness, the gadgets he couldn't work in the kitchen and the skills he never brought to the bed.

My mother played Bingo on the last Thursday of every month. Twelve women gathered at one of their respective homes, rotating in turn throughout the year, eating casseroles and drinking Lipton tea and talking about the tomfoolery of their men.

When Bingo came to our house, my mother asked me to assist with the preparation of bologna and cream cheese roll-ups. We stabbed the small pieces of meat with toothpicks and set them out on a platter.

Tremolo

In 1994, all the talk at Bingo concerned Lucky Vanous, the formerly obscure actor who came to light as a well-muscled construction worker in a Diet Coke commercial. The script was simple: a group of forty-something female office workers huddled at their corporate window to watch Lucky take his daily Diet Coke break. As he stripped off his sweaty shirt and leaned against the wall in his dirty jeans, the women ogled him shamelessly while a singer's voice crooned, "*I just wanna make love to you!*"

I had seen the commercial many times, and my most common response was a cringing embarrassment for the women involved—the women in the office, and those women there in my living room, cackling about the "washboard stomach" of one of *People* magazine's newest-named beauties. What's more: They longed to draw me into their conversation.

At the time, I was fourteen, a freshman in high school, wanting very much to be wanted and wondering secretly, shamefully, if I would ever find a man attractive. It was clear I was supposed to. It was clear something was supposed to happen to my body when I watched Lucky Vanous drink that Diet Coke. But the feeling was also one of indignation that I would recognize many years later, sweating in the motored snow globe of that Ohio winter, when Kinnell's speaker peruses his lover's body and muses on its universal beauty. Is objectification any less objectification if there is love involved? Or is his unsolicited visual caress—remember, she does not yet know that he is watching—simply another form of voyeurism, or normalized desire, like the women leering from the office window or the women once removed at their television sets?

In other words: *Is objectification any less objectification when women perform it upon men?*

Among the women in my mother's Bingo club were seven wives, several divorcées, a widow whose husband had hung himself from a tree in the local churchyard, and a bright, warm, self-effacing grade school teacher named Jo Ann.

Jo Ann had never married, and she lived with her parents in the same house where she was raised. When it was Jo Ann's turn to host Bingo, the party was held at another player's home, with Jo Ann providing the food and prizes. She traveled, she worked out at a gym, and she seemed to take better care of herself and enjoy her life more than any of the other women there. I admired Jo Ann, always looked forward to seeing her, and was pleased to learn we shared the same birthday.

One evening, when several of the "Bingo girls"—as they were fond of calling themselves—had come over for tea with my mother, I overheard a clandestine conversation:

"Do you really think . . . ? Oh, surely not!"

"She's Catholic, for God's sake!"

"I'm just repeating what was intimated to me," my mother replied. "It's not that I think she'd ever *act* on it, but one does wonder when a perfectly viable, likable woman never goes out on any dates."

"That we *know* of!" Another voice interjected with a cackle.

"Are you saying you think she sees women on the side?"

"No, of course not! I think she sees *men*, but unlike the rest of us, she's more private about it. She'd probably rather elope than go to the trouble of announcing that she'd met Mr. Right."

"Or *Ms.* Right." And there was the ominous cackle again, followed by a round of laughter.

I had never considered until that moment the possibility that someone I knew—remember, I did not yet know myself—might be a lesbian. I felt frightened at the thought but also intrigued. Did it mean something that Jo Ann was my favorite of my mother's friends? Did it mean something that I felt most comfortable with her, as if I knew and understood her best? Should I be concerned that we were both September 5 Virgos, as if something in our mutual stars had marked us for an unconventional future?

Somewhere in my mind, I decided that the lesbian speculation must be true, and this secret certainty came to provide an unexpected comfort. Jo Ann was *one of those women*, and she still lived a good life. Of course, she would have to be celibate—anything else was unthinkable—but at least she had her travels and her books and a membership at a top-notch gym.

But then the Lucky Vanous business began, and Jo Ann was just as eager as everyone else to discuss his body, to agree that "they didn't make men like that anymore, and it's a crying shame!" and to speculate about what kind of woman had snared him. "Now *she's* the lucky one," someone quipped, and the whole room thundered with guffaws.

I brought the bologna and cream cheese roll-ups, and I refilled the glasses of André champagne, all the while gazing at Jo Ann with something akin to disappointment, something resembling reproach. *Shouldn't she be different?* I thought. The other women, it was plain, didn't know any better; they responded to the Lucky Vanous commercial the same way their husbands and exes would have responded to a *Sports Illustrated* swimsuit calendar set out on the penny ante poker table. Maybe for most of them it was performance anyway: behaving as you're supposed to behave, mimicking the women in the office window because they represent *your* demographic after all, and you wouldn't want anyone having the conversation about you that you had been having about Jo Ann.

I wanted Jo Ann to be different. It seemed, back then, that I needed her to be. As I took up the small TV trays and gathered the crumpled napkins in a bag, one of my mother's friends called out to me, "Honey, have you seen this Lucky Vanous we're all swooning over?"

I shook my head. I didn't want to participate.

"Of course you have," my mother interceded. "He's that incredible hunk from the Diet Coke commercials." *Hunk?* She had to be kidding.

"Oh, yeah, I guess I have."

"And what do you think—isn't he dreamy?"

"I don't know . . . I guess I'd have to know something more about him."

"Like his street address!" the cackler interjected from across the room.

"No, like whether he was kind or not, whether he had a brain in his head . . . " And all my muscles got very tight like a balloon stretched close to bursting.

"With abs like that, who needs brains?" someone else exclaimed, and once again, their laughter ricocheted from wall to wall.

~

Angie is teaching Dickinson to her students in Advanced Placement literature this semester. A full-time librarian, she also fills many fissures in the school's curriculum, including the lack of AP classes. I stand in the doorway, then wander to where she sits, her hair pinned up, studying.

"Dickinson, eh?"

"You Canadian now?"

Sinking into the sofa cushions, I recite aloud: "*Wild nights - Wild nights! Were I with thee Wild nights should be Our luxury!*"

"But you *are* with me," she smiles.

"So I shall be a virgin recluse no longer."

~

For many years, I lived as a virgin recluse. I knew that terrain. No man had inspired in me any of the emotions evoked by a poem or literary passage. And if love couldn't be as good as books, I wasn't sure I wanted it after all.

But if I were to attempt to transcend the hypothetical again, I knew the next man would have to be larger. I stood five feet ten inches tall, with broad shoulders and muscular thighs. I couldn't stand next to a man who made me feel like an ogre, above whom I loomed like a tree. And so when I met Charlie, all six feet four inches of him, with broad hands and big feet and a width that promised I would be safely eclipsed, I cannot say a certain physical profiling did not take place. I cannot say I was without ulterior motives.

Now at last the lesbian speculation could end. Now at last I could become a woman with an appropriate relationship to men.

"I don't know where you get your ideas," my father often said, "but at this rate, no man is ever going to call twice."

"That's OK, Dad. I don't care if they ever call once."

But the truth was, I *did* care. I saw other girls going out on dates, getting engaged, and Kirsten, my closest friend, had gotten married and moved to California with her husband. It might as well have been Ohio, for all I was going to see her again.

So in part, yes, it was about Kirsten and wanting to follow in her shiny footsteps, which seemed always to know where they were going. My mother had met my father selling shoes and married him by the time she was twenty-two. Now I was twenty-one, selling shoes and finishing my final year of school. Charlie was thirty-one, a walking oxymoron of red suspenders, black business suit, and Fonzie-style leather jacket.

With Charlie, I did not become myself. I became the woman in the Kinnell poem whose voice is never heard and whose actions are interpreted always in light of her interpreter's desire. This is not to say that I did not, in many ways, aspire to be that woman—adored and praised, though notably for her beauty, not her brains.

I come back to that first beloved passage now and read it again in context: the woman and man in afterglow, *him like the big, folded wings of her.* Kinnell likens the lovers to a woodcock in camouflage, lingering at length in one place until the outside world intrudes and sends the bird scurrying. The image of the woodcock is a strange one here, though the reference to camouflage is fitting. I suppose I was once a skittish little bird hoping to hunker in a nest of someone else's making. Flight seemed such a terrifying prospect, and I had found in Charlie someone loyal, someone who was not about to leave me but who in fact was looking for a reason to settle down.

Charlie and I might have stayed as we were, him traveling three hours north to be with me over long weekends in graduate school. I was always happy to see him come, yet grateful to let him go, surprising myself with the delight I took in tidying my apartment after his departure. I had read a poem by Robert Hass in poetry class called "Meditation at Lagunitas," and I was fond of writing a line from it on the flap of envelopes I sealed with a kiss and sent to Charlie: *Longing, we say, because desire is full of endless distances.*

It seemed a sweet sentiment at the time, recognizing that we lived in different cities then, but this did not change our devotion to each other. For me, in fact, the distance made it easier, as it allowed me to conjure Charlie more as I wanted him to be and less as he actually was. Now when I think of those words, I consider their ominous subtext, the distance between us that we could not fill, inexplicable though it was, though it remained. It is not enough to say that the woman I was could not have embraced love with a man. She did embrace it, however awkwardly. She superimposed herself onto those love poems and stretched out in the woman's form against the man, eager and adoring. But as something startles the woodcock, something startled her also. She learned there was a safe inside her body or mind, hinged perhaps at their meeting place along the spine, for which a complex combination was pending.

~

"Do you know the first time I saw you—I mean, really *saw* you—was Valentine's Day?"

Angie thinks I'm being romantic again and remembering it all wrong.

"No, see, you didn't see me, but I saw you. Charlie and I were walking back to my apartment after dinner in Sehome Square. We passed the Birnam Wood Apartments, where you were living then—"

"Well, at least that part is accurate."

"I looked up, and you were standing in the laundry room by the window that faced the road—you know the one—and you were the only person there, or at least the only person I could see, and you were looking down, poignantly, and I felt something for you that I had never felt for Charlie, in all those months together. You were just a girl from grad school I'd hardly spoken to, but—"

"—you would have loaned me quarters if I'd asked you?"

"Something like that," curling into the crook of her arm. "Yes, something like that, I suppose."

~

I learned also that it was harder than it looked to pose. I had become moderately adept at the sex of accommodation, where my body became a means to a man's end. The problem was that he also wanted to please me, which required my capitulation to pleasure and my performance of it.

For Valentine's Day, as with other holidays preceding, I received the usual doting card and a gift-wrapped box containing what I referred to as "mannequin wear." Not in front of Charlie, though, for I didn't want to hurt his feelings. Instead, I would smile at the lacey things—bras and panties and this time, a pair of old-fashioned black garters with buttons and hooks.

"Remember the black boots I bought you for your birthday?" I *did* truly love those. "Well, now you have something to wear them with." He winked. "Go try this on."

One of the ways I knew with certainty, at the age of twenty-two, that I was not a lesbian was because I could not muster any excitement for the bodies of women in Victoria's Secret commercials. They may as well have been Lucky Vanous for all the interest I showed. Of course, I understood that they were beautiful in that polished, mannequin way, but not once had I been stirred by the image of long legs in high heels strutting a runway, or even by the voluminous white wings that extended and ensconced their willowy silhouettes.

Now Charlie wanted me to be one of them, or to do my best, and I tried doggedly to comply. I should have asked him why my getting dressed again with the garters and the black boots and all the lacey things underneath brought him such pleasure. I had no equivalent in my life for the instant erection, but I could transport myself to another place while he undressed me. I could think of something simple and without ceremony, like leaves blowing or snow falling or a stranger riding her bicycle down a long, winding road. It saddened me to think that many women before me had also practiced some version of *close your eyes and think of England*. I had judged them for their coldness, for their inability to find the love in lovemaking, the raw, ecstatic joy. But there I was, being made love to—that ridiculous, if also fitting, masculine phrase—and there was no tremolo in my body, just some version of the even keel: neither joy nor pain, neither hope nor fear. I carried inside me a quiet acceptance that this was what love was going to mean for me: a notch on the tree of longing somewhere between the hard labor of splitting wood and the word-bliss of playing Scrabble.

The image of Angie, with her downturned eyes and small, precise mouth, also sprang readily to mind.

~

Now Angie reads the poems by Galway Kinnell and declares when she's done: "These are terrible."

"But he's an accomplished poet," I protest. "That can't be the end of your analysis."

"Why not? It isn't that the man can't string some words together, can't craft an image. But the gaze is landlocked. It's all body, nothing more . . . and it's *her* body, except for the one place where he works in about his penis. Most importantly, the narrative is boring. Nobody wants to read a we-just-made-love poem or a we're-just-about-to-make-love poem."

But we *do* want to read those poems, or at least we read them, willing or not, and some of us have needed them as a kind of touchstone for what sex is, for what it might be when all is working together for good, when love and pleasure are in attendance, longings fully acknowledged. Yet the whole inquest—the reason I had sought to revisit the Kinnell poems again after so many years—was because I sensed that something in the love poem, or the making-love poem, or both, was working against me, was perhaps even colluding with my unconscious mind to encourage my participation against myself.

I met Angie in graduate school. We studied together for our comprehensive exams. At the time, we both loved a particular poem, the one I mentioned, "Meditation at Lagunitas" by Robert Hass. Yes, it is a beautiful poem, an intelligent poem, a poem that seems to burst upon the page in a single explosion of insight without the need for or possibility of revision. Yes, I have loved this poem and continue to cherish it even now, even as I fear I may have outgrown it.

The poet-speaker recalls, *There was a woman I made love to* (his action upon her, however tender . . .) *and I remembered how holding her small shoulders in my hands sometimes* (she is smaller than he, he is larger than she, they are as they should be . . .), *I felt a violent wonder at her presence like a thirst for salt* (that impossible, imperfect thirst, which is at the heart of Kinnell's poems also—to possess her completely). Thinking of this woman leads the speaker through a fractured retrospective, his salient moments and his commonplace ones. She opens the vault for him, and inside he finds . . . himself, just as he always knew he would.

Hass is more honest perhaps than other poets because his speaker admits, *It hardly had to do with her.*

⁓

How much does the person we love, or the person with whom we pantomime love, have to do with us—the lovers, the ones who tell this kind of story and hold this kind of gaze? I never knew that women could hold the gaze until they were craning their necks out an office window to stare at a bare-chested construction worker, or looking up from the meatloaves they were pounding to view the same scene on their boxy Magnavox TVs. But when women are gazing, do we become men somehow, since it was from men that we first acquired this love of looking?

It is hard for me to tell you how much I love Angie without *tracing her long neck, the tantalizing line of her*, without mentioning her *downturned eyes and small, precise mouth*. This says nothing, of course, of her brilliance, or of her dry wit, or of her tenderness, which has been the real grace of my life. But to give a glimpse of her—the physical incarnation—allows me to move beyond abstraction. It allows me a truer vantage from which to account for my story.

~

Remember the safe with its combination pending? All the numbers needed to align precisely and in correct succession, and when that occurred, I could no longer deny what I actually wanted.

At some point in my courtship with Charlie, it became clear that I did not love him or that I loved him to a lesser degree. Not coincidentally, this epiphany contained a parallel truth, an oyster bearing two pearls. It became clear to me also that I loved Angie, a woman I did not know well but with whom my extensive camouflage was readily cast off and in whose presence my body responded with delight.

The trouble was that I had no way to love her, no physical means to express my desire without falling back on what I had learned from men. My entire life seemed a Rubik's cube of failed matches, of colors that would not come together in a pleasing, monochrome row. I had not been able to enjoy being objectified. I had not been able to rejoice in my power to incite a man's desire. (*It hardly had to do with me.*) Instead, I was always fulfilling a role: the lesbian thespian desperate for a method, the private detective working love from the inside.

It so happened that I was taking a fiction elective at the time, and my teacher was one of only three out lesbians I had met in my life at that time. She assigned us a book called *Valencia* written by Michelle Tea—a queer poet, novelist, and activist from San Francisco. This would be my independent research project. I would study the way that women loved each other. I would take an abstract notion and give it heart and hands.

Imagine me in my khakis, my blue jeans with gold seams, my knit sweaters and crinkly windbreakers. Imagine me teaching a morning composition class, then walking down Holly Street in bayside Bellingham, clasping my cloth shoulder bag with the punk dyke memoir burning a hole inside.

I went to La Vie en Rose bakery every day for a combination breakfast/lunch. I sat on a high stool facing the window and drank coffee from a tall cup and ate a crusty roll stuffed with tomato, avocado, and provolone. I liked the easy routine and aesthetic presentation.

Then, I opened *Valencia*, and it was a like a swarm of hungry bees spilling out in immeasurable quantities. These weren't honeybees like the kind I knew. These weren't Sunday afternoon, bustling-among-the-roses bees. I was terrified. I could hardly breathe, but it was unthinkable to put this book down: *All those girls knew Petra was taking me home to fuck me. They probably knew more about it than I did, in terms of what to expect . . . I stretched the white clingy glove over my fingers, and I slid them one, two, three, four, up her cunt.* Put your fist up me. *What? I had read about this once, in a lesbian book.* Your fist. *God, the energy shooting off her chest was intense, she was a ball of electricity. This was the girl for me.*

If Michelle Tea was the ingenue in this story, there was no word for what I was. Beyond naive, beyond any other delicate sounds the French have concocted to describe an all-consuming cluelessness, a paralyzing lack of prodigy where matters of the flesh are concerned. But there was something else I noticed, amid confusion and fascination and fear: Tea observes, *Petra was really into the knife. I got the sense that I could have been any body beneath her, it was the knife that was the star of the show.*

Apart from the knife, I understood this sentiment precisely. I had convinced myself it was a purely heterosexual problem, a woman becoming generic for a man. But maybe the phenomenon was unsexed after all; maybe the real culprit was power.

I thought how, in sex with a man—and this was the only kind of sex I knew—the penis always took precedent. (And what was the knife, of course, but another phallic symbol? I had learned at least that much in my first psychology class.) It seemed that sexual activities, of which I had discovered intercourse was only one (perhaps the most boring one . . .), were typically organized around a phallus, what Tea had characterized as *the star of the show.* But I had concluded prior to reading her book that sex was a male-centered activity, which explained our phallocentric syntax—make love *to*—with women as the object of the prepositional phrase.

Here, in Tea's story, I found the rebuttal. Tea was going *to be fucked* by Petra, and by many other girls as the origami of the plot unfolded. Hers was simply a rawer way of saying the same things poets like Kinnell and Hass were saying. Women in their poems were made love to; women in *Valencia* got fucked.

But then of course, they were all women in *Valencia*, which meant some of them were doing the fucking also, wielding knives and dildos, pursuing and wooing and Midas-like, turning the bodies of others from cool skin to orgasmic gold.

Because we are all narcissists some of the time, and decidedly narcissists in love, I wanted to understand only what *Valencia* meant for me. I didn't care about Michelle Tea or Petra or any of the other girls. I wanted to know what I had to do to love Angie, to make her or let her love me. Did one of us have to play the man, even symbolically? In the absence of a phallus, so many proxies had been invented for us, striped and solid, glittery and plain. Did we need these? Was there no way to unravel such typecast and overburdened roles?

My heart sunk deep in my stomach, and the food didn't taste good anymore. It was that feeling of profound disappointment, like looking forward to a secret and then finding you have heard it before. Everything happened faster in *Valencia*, faster and harder and answering to different names, but the differences I feared were merely semantic, and the story in the end proved quite the same.

I didn't know if I could be a lesbian. I felt quietly disqualified. And now, instead of just a failing heterosexual, I would be recast as a failed queer.

~

"What's your favorite poem?" I ask Angie. We are making dinner in the slender white kitchen of our faculty apartment.

"Well, I like Prufrock. You know that. I'm teaching it in AP Lit next week."

"I like Prufrock, too. I like especially when he says, *Do I dare disturb the universe?*"

Angie glances at the recipe absently, knowing it already by heart. "If he wants to love, I suppose he'll have to let his universe be disturbed."

"Not to mention his image of himself."

And, of course, I was talking about me again, remembering how I, too, had once measured out my life with coffee spoons—my flawless organization, my clear preference for the hypothetical over the actual. Then suddenly, that meticulously polished Big Picture devolved into kaleidoscope, and every fractured image was a version of Angie's face.

"And *your* favorite poem?" Angie prods, knowing I want her to ask.

"It's not my favorite for all time, but I'd have to say Cisneros, sometimes, 'Bay Poem from Berkeley'."

"Is that the one where she sleeps with the bed full of books?"

"Yes," I say, contentedly stirring. "And at the end she confesses, *These mornings I wish books loved back.*"

~

Once, I had the folly to wonder whether love could ever be as good as books. I mistook my own body for a safe someone else should open, the trousseau a possession I could never actually possess. And I believed Kirsten when she told me the love poem was a travelogue from a place everyone wanted to visit. Perhaps it's true, but love's not the same place for every person. We start to change things from the moment we arrive, altering borders, nudging the static shape of a lumpy nugget state like Ohio, or the one before that—Pennsylvania—or the one before that—Washington—where my own rapturous journey first began.

~

That day in graduate school, when I turned over the first page of my comprehensive exam, Angie was sitting beside me in the stuffy computer lab. We had lived together eight months then. We wore sentimental silver rings on our hands. We had disturbed the universe and lived to tell about it. Then this:

Q1. Please identify the excerpt below and write a thoughtful analysis of its content.

> *The world tells me I am its creature*
> *I am raked by eyes   brushed by hands*
> *I want to crawl into her for refuge   lay my head*
> *in the space   between her breast and shoulder*
> *abnegating power for love*
> *as women have done   or hiding*
> *from power in her love   like a man*
> *I refuse these givens   the splitting*
> *between love and action   I am choosing*
> *not to suffer uselessly   and not to use her*
> *I choose to love   this time   for once*
> *with all my intelligence*

The lines were from "Splittings," the final passage of a famous poem by Adrienne Rich. This was a poem I had needed so many years before, but perhaps it came from a place where I was not yet ready to travel. In a few moments, I would have to begin writing in a formal, scholarly way about the poetic speaker's resolve and the significance of her resolution. But just then I wanted to revel in her words: *abnegating power for love as women have done.* What a wondrous word this *abnegation*! How perfectly it captured the feminine ascetic, desperate to be desired at any cost. I thought of Kinnell and Hass and others, men whose poems acted as distractions from the real power they held, the inequities that undergirded their speakers' love. How bold was Rich to *refuse these givens*, to leave the Rubik's cube on the coffee table and renounce the games of cat-and-mouse, show-and-tell, stone-and-martyr.

What would it mean, I wondered, to love at last with all my intelligence? What would it mean if we weren't expected to abandon our minds, be literally *out of our minds*, in order to love? I wanted to revise the notion that folly is a prerequisite for passion, the belief that we must forsake our better selves in order to find our best partner. Maybe that was the real work ahead, for my life on and beyond the page.

For Angie, for the next book I write, or the next book I give, this inscription— *It always had to do with you.*

Still Life with Guns

For Dr. James Holloway

- The first time they fired a gun at a track meet, I dropped to my knees. I was seven. I had bony knees. Most likely, they were crusted with scabs from bike rides and tree climbs gone awry. Still, I dropped to my knees instead of sprinting the fifty-yard dash. I wore my black nylon shorts and my bright blue shirt that read WEST SEATTLE STRIDERS in shiny letters. But I could not stride, not then. I brought shame on my team as I buckled: down on my knees, hands over my ears. The coach was screaming from the sidelines, but I didn't care. I heard "On your mark!" I heard "Get set!" I was waiting for "Go!" No one said, "Go!" No one ever mentioned a gun.

- Until the late 1950s, teen-sleuth Nancy Drew was allowed to borrow her father's car and his gun. I loved these books late into the 1980s, but this fact seemed to me the very essence of permissive parenting. Once, Nancy Drew was hit with the blunt end of a revolver. She dropped to the floor, unconscious. *Still,* I thought, *how much better than being shot.*

- My parents did not keep guns. No one in our suburban neighborhood had been the victim of violent crime. We lived in a "safe place" by all accounts. I had no reason to believe otherwise. And yet, for many years, I dreamed that a man came to our door and rang the bell. We could see his shadow through the frosted glass. When we didn't answer, he pelted the lock with bullets. The door fell down. Then, he stood in the hallway, backlit by a streetlamp. He wore a wool cap stretched over his face. He was tall and lean with clean jeans and gloves. He pointed the gun at my father, my mother, and me. He shot us, one by one.

- Once, on *Silver Spoons*, Ricky's grandfather took him hunting. This was 1984, which means I was too young to be watching. Maybe I saw a rerun. I still remember the deer. Ricky doesn't want to kill him—a strong buck with antlers as intricate as the cat's cradle game we played with yarn. Someone takes the yarn from someone else's fingers. You have to be careful so everything doesn't collapse. The deer collapses on the hard ground. For years, I see him on his buckled legs, the hole in his side, the blood.

- Once, my father gave me a cap gun. He said it reminded him of when he was a boy in Montana, playing Cowboys and Indians. That was the 1940s. They didn't know any better then. The gun he gave me was black and silver with a long, slender barrel. It came with a jeweled holster ("for cowgirls!") and a pack of coiled red paper called caps. My father loaded the paper into the gun and told me to fire. "It doesn't matter where. You can't hurt anything." Then, he reconsidered: "Well, don't point it at your face." I clicked the trigger and smelled smoke. I liked the smell but not the feel of the trigger under my finger. Mostly, the gun stayed in the holster after that.

- "If you have the dream again," my father said, exhausted, slumped against the side of my bed, "we will have to stop reading *Nancy Drew*. It's putting ideas in your head." I did have the dream again, so I continued reading *Nancy Drew* in secret.

- I used to have water guns in all different colors. My friends and I shot at each other in the swimming pool and running through the sprinklers. Someone we knew even had a Super Soaker. We squealed and shouted "Stop!" but we didn't mean it. We were trigger-happy. We made shooting noises. We cast great arcs of water across the lawn. "Gotcha! Gotcha!" we cried. But no one ever fell down or writhed on the ground. No one ever pretended to be dead.

- My parents sat me down and explained that I was not allowed to take the toy gun I didn't play with outside of our backyard. There had been a shooting in the city—a real one. A little boy was waving a toy gun in an alley after dark. A policeman called out for whoever was there to drop his weapon and put his hands in the air. (I was not even allowed outside after dark. I didn't even know where I would find an alley.) The boy thought they were playing a game. He kept waving the gun the way you might wave one of those toys you get at the circus. Maybe it *was* one of those toys—a Ringling Brothers sparkling ray gun, let's say. The boy never put it down, and the policeman shot him dead. Later—I can't be sure if I dreamed this or not—the policeman apologized to the dead boy's family on television. Parents were told to talk to their children about guns. My parents only repeated what they had already said.

- In *The Sound of Music,* Liesl's boyfriend Rolf pulls a gun on Liesl's father, Captain von Trapp. I am terrified every time this happens. "You'll never be one of them," the Captain says, taking the gun from Rolf's hand. How does he know Rolf won't pull the trigger? The very next moment, Rolf blows his whistle, exposes them all. More troubling still: How could Liesl have danced with this boy, kissed him by lightning glow in her family's gazebo? How could the same hands that held her so gently have also held that gun?

- Once, I went home with Jamie after school. Her father worked nights and slept during the day. We had to be quiet, she told me, over and over, even though I could hear the television blaring behind the bedroom door. Everything in Jamie's house was very white and very clean, but there was a small, dark hole in the wall. I asked her about it. She said her father got angry and fired his BB gun indoors. The next time I came over, a picture hung on that wall.

- At recess one day, we told each other the worst ways to die. Someone was afraid of drowning. Someone was afraid of burning alive. Someone was afraid of falling from the top of a skyscraper. No one was afraid of sharks or freezing to death or zombies. These weren't popular ways to go in 1989. "I'm afraid of being shot," I said. The boys told me I could survive a flesh wound, no problem. I clarified: "I'm afraid of being shot to death." My voice quivered as I said it.

- Once, my grandmother sent me to the cellar for something. Or maybe she didn't. Maybe I was nosing around where I didn't belong, just like I always did. I opened the door and felt a draft rising from under the house. I reached for the frayed string and tugged it twice before the bare bulb over the stairs clicked on. Canning supplies and carpentry tools—that's all anyone said the cellar was good for. I took a couple of steps down, then froze, mid-stair. Leaning against the wall was a rifle, old and unpolished. From a certain angle, you could mistake it for a cane. I did not touch the gun but studied it in the wan light, sizing it up like a schoolyard bully. How I wanted to kick it, to throw it down, but in the end, I left it in darkness.

- Once, at a garage sale, I was trying to help my mother make a "good find." We got there early to rifle through the boxes. She said it like the word wasn't loaded: *rifle* through. We did this a lot. We *rifled*. Usually, there were only a few lockets without chains or a set of chipped teacups or a cloth pouch full of silver dollars, but this time I opened a shoebox full of guns. They were pistols, I guess, like those I had seen on *Perry Mason*. At first, I thought they must be the same as my little cap gun, but when I lifted one out of the box, it was heavy and oily. My wrist bent in an unnatural way. Someone was just selling guns on his front lawn. Anyone could come and buy one. I put the lid back on the box, but all day I felt the slick heft in my hand and wished I could go back and un-feel it.

- Gender and guns go together like this, according to black-and-white movies I grew up watching: If a woman is a lady, she may carry a small revolver with a pearl handle in her purse, purchased for her by a husband or a beau. She may choose to wrap it in a scented handkerchief, or if there is nothing else, a wash rag from her linen closet. If a man is a gentleman, he may wear a shoulder holster under his suit, keep a loaded firearm for just in case. When a man who is not a gentleman steals the purse of a woman who is a lady and then holds her at gunpoint with her own weapon, a man who is a gentleman may approach from behind, wrest the gun from his hand, and save the lady from her almost-certain demise.

- Somewhere the television is always on. The television is always showing a movie. The movie is always a James Bond movie—old Bond, classic Bond—Sean Connery or Roger Moore. Somewhere my father is sitting on the sofa in our basement, his head like a silver bust. The shadow of a man crosses the screen, centered in a sniper's circle. Suddenly, he turns. He points a gun at the sniper, who might as well be my father. The blood falls like a curtain, thick and red. This is what I mean when I think, *James Bond shoots my father every day*, right through the heart. Somewhere I am always watching.

- It was "all in good fun," but I didn't want to play paintball at day camp. I didn't want to carry a gun and run through the woods plucking off kids wearing different-colored bandannas. Yet the counselors insisted: "This is important for team-building." One was a tall woman called Squirrel. The other was a short woman called Inch. They spoke as one voice. They told my mother I was lacking team-building skills, being an only child. She dropped to her knees and pleaded with her eyes: *stop being so difficult.* "What does it hurt?" my mother said. But I shook my head and balled my fists. I would be sick that day—force a fever, scald my hand on purpose. "What does it help?" I replied.

- One Christmas it dawned on me that if George Bailey had really been serious about ending his life, he would have used a gun. Guns were for serious people with serious purposes. Surely God, if there was one, would have known this. Maybe that's why He sent the angel second-class.

- One Fourth of July, I couldn't sleep because the firecrackers sounded like gunshots. The world outside my window was transformed into an Old West saloon. I imagined the gunfights, men in fringed vests taking shots of whiskey, then trying to beat each other to the draw. My father loved Westerns. I imagined the barmaid who brought their next round: her white sleeveless blouse, her small bare shoulders. I took time with her face, care with her body. Once she was real to me, I feared for her deeply. How could she not be caught in the crossfire?

- In 1991, we rented *Regarding Henry* at the video store. I had just turned twelve, but the movie was rated PG-13. My parents decided I was old enough to watch. Henry was a lawyer. Henry was not very likable. Henry was played by the famous Harrison Ford. His wife Sarah was so pretty she made my teeth hurt. Sarah was a mother, but she didn't remind me of mine. Sarah was played by the famous Annette Bening. One night while waiting in line at a convenience store, Henry was shot in the head. There was a robber, a holdup; things went awry. This was my worst fear realized. But Henry didn't die. Instead, he forgot who he was and had to learn to walk, talk, and think all over again. He became an entirely different man—by all accounts, a better man. My parents clapped at the end of the film like we were at the circus. "What did you think?" they wanted to know. "Wasn't that inspiring?" But I couldn't tell them I thought I would never sleep again, let alone set foot inside a 7-Eleven.

- "You're too old to still be having bad dreams," my father chided. He was tired of the way my screams woke him up at night, tired of the way my mother slept right through them. "The things you see on television and in movies—they're all make-believe." He tucked me into bed again. "Just remember that none of it is real."

- Once, my parents took me to see *Annie Get Your Gun* at the Renton Civic Theatre. It's a musical love story based on the real life of Annie Oakley, the sharpshooter from Buffalo Bill's Wild West Show who later fell in love with marksman Frank Butler. We left the theater humming. At home, my mother brought out her sheet music—favorites of Irving

Berlin—and we all stood around the piano singing: *"Oh you can't get a man with a gun!"*

• Guns N' Roses was a popular band at that time. I learned they had an *Appetite for Destruction*. My classmates were listening to their music on cassette tapes with headphones and on the radio in the after-school parking lot. I kept picturing red roses arranged in a bouquet, a black gun splayed across the petals. I did not have a Walkman or a radio, though, and I was not allowed to listen to music of my era.

• Already: Abraham Lincoln, Mahatma Gandhi, Malcolm X, John F. Kennedy, Jr., Che Guevara, Martin Luther King, Jr., Harvey Milk, Medgar Evers, John Lennon, Indira Gandhi, Michael Collins, Marcus Foster. Names that hovered in the history books, resurfaced in the headlines from time to time. Some names I was even tested on in school. Yet to come: Kurt Cobain, Tupac Shakur, Phil Hartman, Gianni Versace, Benazir Bhutto, Selena, Yitzhak Rabin, Tara Correa-McMullen. Also places that would serve as stand-ins for people: Columbine, Newtown, Charleston, Ferguson, Pulse. I spelled "assassination" correctly in a regional spelling bee by remembering that it is "ass" twice followed by "i" and "nation." Later, I won a round with "massacre" by remembering "mass" and "acre" joined, by thinking of the many who share the same land.

• Every morning before sunrise, my mother drove me to the Catholic high school on Capitol Hill. The building loomed like a castle, the lone cross on the turret piercing the fog. On our way, we passed the coed public high school and a community swimming pool where girls from my school practiced their strokes before class. In the afternoons, my father drove up the long hill and brought me home. Sometimes there was a swim meet at the Medgar Evers pool. Sometimes I saw the Holy Names van parked outside. If I listened closely, I could even hear the starter's pistol, followed by the synchronized splash.

• Sophomore year our teacher's husband killed himself. We prayed for him at mass, even though it was too late. We also prayed for her. I was not sure if this helped or hurt or did anything at all. I remembered seeing them together once, chaperoning a dance, how happy they looked only two months before his death. I wrote about the incident in my first book: the husband who took a lethal dose of pills, the wife who thought he was sleeping in their bed. Years later, I reunited with a friend who told me, "You got everything wrong. He drove out to the mountains alone, in the brutal cold, far from everyone. He put a gun in his mouth and swallowed the bullet." Either way, he was dead. Either way, his wife was widowed. And yet, somehow, my version of this story was easier to bear.

- Sophomore year, a freshman at the coed public high school left a Martin Luther King, Jr. Day assembly, walked home, grabbed a nine-millimeter semi-automatic handgun, and returned to school to confront a junior who had bullied and robbed him: *My plan was to get him to come with me, like to a bathroom. Do some TV shit like put [the gun] in his mouth and make him strip down. Get my stuff back, take any money he had on him, then leave him buck naked inside the boys' bathroom as an example to everybody else: "Don't fuck with me." And then it would be cool.*

- Sophomore year, a TV show about a high school girl—also a sophomore—named Angela Chase premiered on MTV. She was fifteen, like me. Her life was *so-called*, like mine. Angela Chase attended a coed public high school where, in the third episode, her friend Ricky's cousin brought a gun to school, hoping to sell it. The gun went off by accident, piercing a locker and the can of soda inside. Ricky's cousin peed his pants and ran away. Soda added to the dangerous slick of the floor. In response to parental outrage, metal detectors were installed at the main door of the high school as a precautionary measure. Angela's mother said she thought Angela wasn't worried about being shot at school because, like all teenagers, she believed she was immortal. This was where we differed. I never thought I was immortal, not for one moment, ever.

- I still have nightmares, but now I dream of being chased by villains en masse and anonymous. They snipe at me from low-flying planes (shades of *North by Northwest*) and town cars with darkened windows (shades of *The Godfather*). I run as fast as I can, but always in the wrong direction. Sometimes when I reach my parents' house, they are already dead, killed execution-style with terrifying efficiency. I grieve that I could not save them. Other times when I arrive at their house, a gnawing intuition purports it is my parents peeping through the curtains, my parents wielding the unseen guns. This grief is more complicated. I grieve that they cannot save me from themselves.

- My small liberal arts college lurked at the base of a mountain. It was a good school in a sketchy valley. The campus sprawled—green, manicured anomaly—amid pawn shops and adult entertainment stores. The neighborhood was hard to explain to parents paying upward of twenty grand each year for their children's clean, safe Christian education. To this end, the campus police made tireless promises: "Students, we will drive you anywhere within a five-mile radius, free of charge. Call for return trip pickup, also free of charge." Meanwhile, a huge yellow banner on the main highway bellowed GUNS FOR SALE at everyone, coming or going. At the college, we joked about it, saying: "Meet you at the welcome sign!"

- When *American Beauty* came to the cinema near my school, I was first in line at the ticket window. I'd read about this film. I knew it was the story of a mother, father, and daughter who lived in a suburb of Any-where, USA. The mother was a master gardener, like my mother, grow-ing those roses all the time. She was played by Annette Bening, who felt different to me then—more like a mother, I suppose. "She's more your mother than he is your father," my friend whispered from the back row. But there were key differences, too—like Mrs. Burnham sold real estate and Mrs. Burnham drove an SUV and Mrs. Burnham was having an affair. In fact, she had just had sex with the "Real Estate King" when he told her how whenever he felt stressed and needed to unwind, he liked to fire a gun. He suggested she should try it, go with him to the firing range, which she did: "Nothing makes you feel more powerful . . . well, almost nothing," he grinned. This was the first time I could recall guns and sex being mentioned in the same breath. It would not be the last.

- In London my junior year, I lived with a host family. This was a popular cliché for students of my demographic, and even more cliché was the fact I didn't know it was. One day my host mom confided in me quiet-ly, as if confessing a crime, that she had been to the States before. "It's not that I didn't enjoy myself," she said, "and the children loved your Disney World. But the whole time I was in your country, I couldn't stop wondering how American parents cope with the fear." I wasn't sure what she meant. "I think the rides are pretty safe," I offered. "Oh, not the rides—just life in general. Aren't your parents afraid every day that you'll be shot?"

- Like all white, middle-class, American college students studying abroad in England, I went to Ireland for spring break. What made me different was that I didn't drink much or often, while most of my peers went for the St. Patrick's Day parties. *American Beauty* was playing in the small, coastal town of Bray. I bought a ticket and hunkered down alone in the dark. This time I thought about my father, who was really nothing like Lester Burnham, it's true. In the voiceover prologue, he told viewers he'd be dead in six months. We forgot. Things seemed to be going well for Lester Burnham. He was smoking pot and pumping iron and enjoying his nice severance package. We were happy for Lester Burnham. He got the audience in the imminent divorce. Then, his neighbor stormed into his house with a shotgun and, just as the saying goes, blew his brains out. Lester Burnham was dead then. We couldn't forget. The blood flowed from the counter in a thick, red curtain.

- I remember a kid in an airport once, watching the adults around him react to a shooting on the news. He pulled his hoodie down and glanced from face to stricken face. "It's still life!" he said. "We're still living!" he shouted. The kid couldn't have been more than thirteen. "It's just that it's life with guns."

- In 1991, a graduate student at the University of Iowa killed four professors and one classmate before turning the gun on himself. Five years later, a woman who knew these people, worked with them every day—a woman who might have died herself if things had gone differently—published an essay called "The Fourth State of Matter." In another five years, I would be assigned to read this essay for a class in graduate school. During the late-night quiet, I would weep so long and so hard that something seemed to shatter inside me.

- May 17, 2001. I was about to graduate from college and head off to graduate school. By all accounts, I had had a clean, safe, Christian education. I was only a little bit deflowered. In some words, I had been sheltered, empowered, intimidated, and inspired. On this day, I was visiting a friend in her dorm. The day was bright and uncharacteristically warm. Students lounged on the lawn, pretending to study for final exams. A work crew was trimming the bushes. On my friend's wall I noticed a poster of Mel Gibson, the word RANSOM printed beneath him, hands set firmly under his chin. "I love his eyes," she said, "how piercing they are." I thought of Rene Russo instead, who played Gibson's wife in the film. She did not remind me of my mother. "What *Ransom* doesn't show is how much therapy all those people are going to need after that shoot-out in their home." I was strangely pleased with myself as I said this. Then, a car backfired on a nearby road and instinctively, I ducked for cover.

- On May 17, 2001, a professor at my small liberal arts college was fatally shot by a stranger in the courtyard outside a central dorm. The stranger then turned the gun on himself. Nursing students pretending to study on the lawn performed CPR on both men until an ambulance arrived. The ambulance arrived too late. From the second-floor stairwell, I regarded the bodies: two white men in white shirts with splayed limbs, a black gun on the pavement between them. No one yet knew the sequence of events or the motive for the crime. I only knew that I was safe. The glass around me had not shattered. I watched the spot of blood on one man's chest grow larger and larger. The fear I always carried with me had left my body. I waited for something to replace it, but nothing did.

- I didn't know the victim or the perpetrator of the shooting at my school. The aftermath, as I witnessed it, resembled something I might have seen on *Law and Order*. My psychology professor offered me an extension on the final exam because of the possibility of post-traumatic stress. I took the test with everyone else. I declined the free counseling. Ten days later, as I crossed campus for graduation, roses, en masse and anonymous, began to appear, masking the chalk outlines of bodies beneath the well-trimmed shrubs.

- In graduate school, I met a Navy SEAL who served as a sniper for several years. He had insomnia and constant ringing in his ears. He was a kind man in whose presence I always felt safe. There was something cautious and gentle about the way he moved through the world. We became friends, then closer friends. I never asked him how many people he had killed. He never volunteered.

- Later, I fell in love with a woman who grew up listening to Carole King, so I listened to Carole King, too. One night I was driving home to the house we shared. It was late, and I was singing along to the music to stay awake. There was a song on the *Tapestry* album called "Smackwater Jack." I always looked forward to this song: the high energy, the spirited beat. This time, as I sang along, I heard the words in my own voice: "*So he shot down the congregation.*" Behind all that pep and verve, I discovered a song about a lone gunman, a shooting in a church. How had I sung these lyrics so many times but never really heard them until now? King crooned about the man with a shotgun in his hand, and I felt the shame rising in my cheeks.

- Once, I saw a card in a kitschy gift shop with Mae West winking on the cover. Inside the card, the greeting read: "*Is that a gun in your pocket, or are you just glad to see me?*" Once, I saw *I Shot Andy Warhol*, and then I dreamed that I shot Andy Warhol. It was the first time I can recall where my dream cast me as the one committing a crime. Once, I went to a gallery where they were showing the Zapruder film in a constant loop on multiple screens. I wondered if this was how Zapruder felt every day for the rest of his life.

- For one year, I worked as the Public Safety Secretary at a private girls' school in Pennsylvania. Though the campus was small and by all accounts serene, it was patrolled by fourteen police officers who carried loaded handguns in the holsters at their hips. Two were women, one my age. I asked Heather how she felt about firearms. She shrugged. "Probably the same as you feel about pens and paper. They're just what you need to do your job."

- While I was still a student, I had students of my own, and my students were writing about fear. Someone was afraid of snakes. Someone was afraid of carnival rides. Someone was afraid of flunking out of school. There were fears of never marrying and of marrying the wrong person, of heart attacks and airplane crashes, of having children and not having children. "What about weapons?" I asked. "What about random acts of violence? What about guns?" I steadied my voice as I said it. A girl in the front row answered with a wave of her hand: "Oh, yeah, but those are just the givens, you know?"

- "You're afraid of guns because you're a woman and women are taught to fear," my friend said. "And who are they taught to fear? *Men.* And what are men more likely to have? *Guns.*" But this was only half true, I reminded her. Women were taught to fear men, but they were also taught that men were the only ones who could save them. *Walk with the right man at night and you wouldn't be harassed or attacked. But walk with the wrong man at night, or walk alone, and the wrong man might rape and kill you.*

- My father called his poker buddies "those old sons of a gun." He always urged me to "stick to my guns." My mother believed it was better "to jump the gun" than ever to be under it. She was known for planning ahead. My teacher used to say, his lips splitting into a grin: "You know the best kind of gun starts with *be*, and without it, you can never be done."

- Sometimes I think I am not a real woman or that I am less than a real woman because my life is not attached to a man's. Then, I wonder if I really think these things or if I am simply aware that others may think them about me. When the laws changed, and my partner and I were finally eligible to marry, a friendly acquaintance quipped, "Well, at least we know it's not a shotgun wedding!" At least we knew that.

- Once, a student asked me somberly, the concern evident in her eyes: "Do you ever think about what happened at Virginia Tech?" *Yes. All the time.* "Did it ever make you consider doing something else with your life?" *No. Not for one moment, ever.*

- There are thoughts I examined and thoughts I was merely aware of thinking. They dangled in the background of consciousness, like stalactites in a cave: One day, very recently, it dawned on me that I had been bracing all my thirty-six years for someone to take my life with a gun. I was not merely afraid; I seemed to expect it would happen. And when it did, I knew I would plead for my life. This would not help me, though, because I was not married to a man or the mother of his children. I feared in my deepest heart that even if hatred of women like me was not the reason for the gun at my temple, it would be a deciding factor when the trigger was finally pulled.

- Once, in my inbox, an advertisement arrived on behalf of an indoor shooting range in Pompano Beach inviting me to "take aim" with a gun-range package for two.

- Once, on my computer screen, this news story from the *Seattle Times* transported me across the country and fourteen years back in time: *Pacific Lutheran University students call their campus the "Lute Dome"—a tranquil place sheltered from outside troubles. That peace was shattered yesterday afternoon when a gunman walked on campus intent on killing the first staff member he saw. Armed with a 9 mm handgun and a .22-caliber for backup, Donald D. Cowan, 55, spotted James D. Holloway, 40, a beloved music professor and renowned organist, outside a student residence hall about 3 p. m. and fired four rounds, striking him three times in the torso and one time in the head, said Lt. Dave Hall, spokesman for the Pierce County Sheriff's Department. Then Cowan walked up to his prone victim, dropped a 16-page suicide note, put the gun to his own head and pulled the trigger a final time.*

- Once, in my classroom, a student wept openly as another read aloud from Brent Staples's "The Coroner's Photographs": *The coroner describes the wounds in detail. The surgical incision and its grisly clamps are dismissed in a single sentence. The six bullet holes receive one full paragraph each. The coroner records the angle that each bullet traveled through the body, the organs it passed through along the way, and where it finally came to rest. With all this to occupy him, the coroner fails to note the scar on Blake's left hand. The scar lies in the webbing between the thumb and index finger and is the result of a gun accident. A shotgun recoiled when Blake fired it and drove the hammer deep into the web, opening a wound that took several stitches to close.* "Should I stop reading?" he finally asked. A third student looked up from the page. "No. I think we have to see it—what Staples saw. We have to face it. Because even if we stop reading, our silence won't bring his brother back to life."

- Sometimes, Bon Jovi still sings "Shot through the Heart" on the Oldies station, and I sing along, remembering that guns can be a metaphor.

- Sometimes, when driving late at night through the deepest part of the American South, past parking lots where gun racks crown the roof of every pickup truck, my wife and I still request a double room.

- Sometimes, when I see a man in a white shirt, standing on a street corner, I have to blink hard and force the image to reload. Just for a moment, I glimpse it: the hole in his side, the blood.

Meditation 35

five

This year I am more legs than torso. I move as if on stilts, unsteady and tentative, but despite this, I still favor stilts on the playground. This sounds like a nursery rhyme, though it isn't. I like the thimble kind—pink buckets turned upside down, tethered to green straps, ideal for clomping. I am far away without meaning to be. I am harder to reach in play, impossible to reach when I am reading. As I wobble and fall, the other children guffaw. I plunge deeper into the white pools of the page.

It's my candle year: two fawn-brown tapers with a flame on top, a flicker of red in my hair. It's my kite-tail year, the long strings of my lower half tugging me back to earth, my head set comfortably among the clouds. Gravity is never an easy lesson.

My mother answers to many names, Gravity among them. She is my first world, my first lesson in limits. I live in a house made of mother and mortar, bright windows and red brick. My father and I dangle from the ceiling, two look-alike kites intertwined. My mother unrolls us and reels us in.

I have trouble telling right from left, making snowflakes, folding paper cranes, and tying my shoes. "Velcro is not an option," my mother says. All my teeth are tight in my mouth for now, but I am afraid of the big tooth on the kindergarten wall that promises loss is coming. I am reading at a third-grade level, but I have failed my draw-a-person test, so my parents are summoned to school to determine whether I am a wunderkind or a dud. The results prove inconclusive.

I begin to memorize what does not come naturally to me. "Left" is the eye that only sees fog. "Right" is the hand with the lonely freckle, one interpunct under the thumb. "Right" is also whatever my mother says. Soon, she enrolls me in after-school activities. When I swim, I feel as true to my body as the stories we are allowed to believe—God and Jesus and George Washington. When I dance, it is always an act of science fiction.

I love stories, but I do not believe the story of my own body; I never have. I am a meta-child who believes in metaphor. No one has told me yet, but they will: *A comparison wherein one thing is described in terms of another.* I anticipate this definition while sculling on my back in the pool, while hanging limp in jellyfish pose, while learning to bob up and down. I open my eyes underwater and regard the others, my namesakes. I am a girl because I resemble these girls. We are like each other without being the same, stick arms and legs with little bellies jutting forth, beveled promontories. See how we shiver when we are cold? See how our fingers raisin when submerged? But the dry land pronounces our differences.

My wet hair is pinned back, my skin still damp under my leotard. Sometimes my stomach rumbles. On the dance studio floor, we stagger ourselves and spread our legs as far as we can, twelve sets of pink tights and slippers. My feet point forward in a V, and when the teacher comes to widen them, they snap back again like a firmly hinged door. Butterfly: "flutter, flutter." We press our soles together and flap energetically. The other girls' knees come to rest on the floor. "Push them down and hold them there," the teacher tells me. Frog: "Hips flat, bottoms down." The teacher comes around, smoothing our prone bodies with her rolling-pin hands. But I am a pop-up book—no splits for me, no sitting on my knees. Even cross-legged, I tip forward, hunching my shoulders. When we practice our piqué turns, I get dizzy and stumble out of line.

The only other dancer I have ever seen belongs to my music box. She tinkles and twirls until the lid crushes her, mid-pirouette, into silence. I believe she brims with many unnamed longings—happiness and also regret. She is a metaphor, but not only a metaphor.

ten

Now the body is both fact and opinion—I can argue with myself, and a deeper self within me argues back. I am a double digit, an exemplar of binary code.

For my birthday, my father takes me to Silver Coin with forty quarters burning a hole in my bag. I spend everything on games with joysticks and steering wheels. Though my scores are low, I relish the racetrack for its circular nature, the spaceship for its aerial view.

This is the year that older women begin to take my hand and lean in close, whispering that I will "soon become interested in boys." But the truth is, I have been interested in boys for a long time. I study their confidence when faced with physical challenges. I admire their fearlessness in falling and bleeding, the pride they take in their most conspicuous wounds. We are similes, these boys and I, two essentially unlike entities linked by a surprising connection.

Our connection is Mrs. Miller, who has wavy brown hair and a soft, pleasing shape; Mrs. Miller has just turned twenty-five. Everyone likes her, but the boys and I—we like her extra. We vie for her attention daily, one-upping each other with clover bouquets and blackberries picked from the thicket we aren't supposed to cross. She thanks us and smiles, pats our cheeks, and touches our foreheads when she suspects we might be flushed.

I run a fever for all of fourth grade, yet I earn a certificate for perfect attendance. I lie in bed at night and fantasize that Mrs. Miller brings me orange juice and an ice pack.

"1" is the girl in me. She likes dresses all right and is excited about switching from ankle socks to stockings in the spring. She glosses her lips and puckers for the bathroom mirror. She might even agree to wear her Easter bonnet again.

"0" is the boy in me. He likes the idea of kissing, the intimacy of breath and two bodies joined by their tongues. In CPR class, he imagines pressing his warm mouth against a stranger he has pulled safely from the pool. The stranger is always a girl.

When I consent to "going steady" this year, I imagine it will be all kickball and bicycle riding, this boy like the brother I never had. He pushes me on a tire swing and listens while I play piano for his neighbor. But he wants something, too—a corporeal engagement with my body that feels both dangerous and uninspired.

"1" is the mouth that kisses him back under the mistletoe, leaving a little smack of cherry. "1" is the body selected from the audience that night for a spotlight dance with the star of *Cotton Patch Gospel*. She looks pretty, her other self concedes, in the black velvet French dress with the blue satin rose. She discovers she enjoys being twirled and dipped, then praised for being graceful after.

"0" is the same mouth that presses into her pillow at night, dreaming of Mrs. Miller, Mandie Salazar from school, and Agent 99 from *Get Smart*. "0" is the body alone and undressed, examined furtively under the covers. This body is growing so fast it will soon surpass the mother's height, is already head-to-head with the boy. And when they stand together in the basement, trying to recreate her moment of light, he puts his arms around her middle, heaves, tells her he isn't sure that he can lift her up.

In Pioneer Girls on Wednesday nights, she wins at foursquare and tetherball. Her long legs fuse into a single fin. She becomes as fast and fluid as water.

Then, we go in. I am my old self again, careless with the glue and scissors, worse with the needle and thread. "You'll just have to tell your parents you didn't earn your domesticity badge," the troop leader says. This is the closest thing we have to Home Economics, and now I've blown it. For Valentine's Day, I bring my mother a hook-and-eye potholder that promptly unravels in her hand. I give my father an eagle fashioned from dark yarn and stuffed with cotton. "Is this a football or a potato?" he asks.

fifteen

My body is no longer a story. It is a novel—new and long at once. I have starved myself till the clavicles pierce through my skin, then soften the flesh beyond the ledge of thin. I have gone through two rounds on Accutane to become unblemished again. I have shaved my legs so fiercely they bled. The exposition is over, and now the rising action begins.

This new, long world is parsed by a Cartesian seam: girls who live too much inside their bodies, and girls, like me, who live too much inside their heads.

The boys are gone now. They belong to the world beyond us. When I ask her, my mother simply repeats what she has read: "Single-sex schools enable young women to excel as leaders and better prepare them to meet the challenges ahead."

In the promotional video, a girl in a class sweatshirt and loose ponytail sips from her Nalgene water bottle and says, "I appreciate not having boys around. I can really concentrate on my schoolwork without distractions here at Holy Names."

At this, my mother balks at the girl's informal dress. "It's a prep school, not a nunnery, and every young woman should learn to look the part!"

"What does that mean—*look the part*? You make it sound like I'm auditioning for something."

"You are—every day—whether you know it or not."

For this reason, my mother will dress me for the rest of high school. She will choose my clothes and lay them on the rocking chair each night, then meet me in the morning with her mousse, pick, and a diffuser she bought at the mall. She likes "the wet look." There are blazers and blouses from Bill Blass, Liz Claiborne slacks with deep pleats, brown woven belts to match my loafers, and a fleet of dreaded trouser socks. I no longer resemble the other girls. I don't even resemble myself.

Perhaps, in retrospect, I begin running cross-country for the clothes. I have never felt more confident, more the way I imagine a boy must feel, than in my black running shorts, Nike sneakers, and long tank top with the cropped black sports bra underneath. Everything is neat and tight, my body moving forward in one straight line. On our training runs and at our races, sweat is expected, required. I tuck my hair under a ball cap. I swish water around in my mouth and spit it out on the ground, the way I've seen real athletes do.

At the end of the season, my coaches present me with the trophy for "Most Improved." My mother weeps at my bedside over how huge my thighs have become. "You need to stop training," she says, "or they're only going to get bigger and bigger."

Is it the story of my body I begin to doubt or the story my mother has told me about my body? This is also the year she leafs through my biology book before announcing out of the blue: "Girls can't masturbate, you know. There's no point in touching yourself."

My face crimsons at the thought. Was she thinking that I had been thinking about it? At the piano, I press down on the damper pedal with all my might. I make the notes smooth and blurry, string them together like Christmas lights.

On television, we watch shows about virgins and angels and a celibate ranger in Texas. One night there is an episode about a woman who has been raped. I am stunned by her sorrow, the way she mourns for what she can neither name nor replace. I tell my parents, "If I were raped, I would kill myself, no question."

"You don't mean that!" my father cries. But I do. I can only love my body alone and in motion; any touch would seem a trespass now.

A few months later, I am sent home from school with chicken pox. "What a relief!" my mother sighs, bringing me orange juice and an ice pack. "I was so afraid it was your acne coming back."

My symbolic quarantine made manifest: I have time on my hands now, time with a body. My mother leaves me gloves and reminds me not to scratch. Sinking deep in the oatmeal bath, I bless myself and let my fingers wander.

twenty

This is the year I begin to land in my body at last, after years of soaring through space, staying the course, naming myself by proximity to others. Who would I be if I touched down somewhere else?

This is also the year I acquire the Latin phrase *sui generis* and begin to cite it as defense and explanation for all my actions. I am not "similar to" or "different from" anyone; I am *sui generis*, I say, end of story.

"Just what is that supposed to mean?" my father demands.

"Unique, peculiar, one of a kind."

Without asking my parents' permission, I apply to have my scholarship transferred to a college in London. I want to hear the language I think I know made new again, and this, too: I want to undo the deep repression that has kept me chaste and fearful, erratic in my acts of longing and withdrawal.

My mother packs my suitcase, selects my clothes for the overnight flight. "Why are you doing this to us?" she keeps asking, and even *sui generis* doesn't seem a suitable response.

First, it is dark, and I am dozing in the back row. Then, the sun is rising over the left wing, and I step into the lavatory to wash my face, to meet my own eyes in the mirror. They are dark blue, often mistaken for brown. The right one, which can see clearly, appears larger than the other—wide awake and ever-watchful.

I look down at the yellow cardigan with little pearl buttons my mother has purchased for me. Do I tug absently at a loose thread? Do I fasten a button that has come undone? Or is the moment more telekinetic than that? Suddenly, they are falling like raindrops into the sink, an insistent clatter of six, seven, eight. The sweater, now buttonless, swings open. I see my ugly beige bra, the same one my mother wears. I see my bare midriff, never flat enough to meet my standards. I gather the pearls and tuck them into my pocket. Even if I could sew, I would still scatter them like ashes.

The body knows something about hyperbole, and the body knows something about hiding. I am cordial with my host family, and they are cordial with me. I stop drinking coffee and convert enthusiastically to tea. Every morning I run the streets of Eastcote, past the red mailboxes and the zebra crossings. I am a portrait of health and good humor. Sometimes I ride the Circle line for hours, writing to the rhythm of the train.

All this to learn: I have come 4,700 miles, and the gnawing in my lower abdomen, the slight constriction under my ribs, never goes away. Rather, it intensifies. I try less wine, more wine, vary my quantities of cider. I take up smoking but try not to inhale. I imagine my pink lungs from the health class diagram, floating now in charcoal clouds.

One morning I notice a church near the house where I stay. The organ music is not as soothing as it is familiar, but it will do. From the back pew, I listen to the minister, trying to place his accent until I realize, disappointed, that it's the same as mine. Afterward, he introduces himself and reveals that he too was raised in Washington. His wife brings me a glass of champagne. For several weeks, I take Christ's body broken for me as I haven't done in years. At least this is something to tell my parents when I call them from the phone box on the corner and promise I'm having a *sui generis* time.

"Come out with us to the club," a classmate cajoles. I wear a short skirt and a red shirt, paint my lips and slick back my hair. A friend from home has sent me a SARK book and I attempt to imitate her "bodacious" style. At the door, a man traces his hand the length of my leg, asks where I've been all his life. It's then I recognize this feeling in my gut: it isn't acid reflux; it's how my mother told me all good girls feel when they lie.

I never go inside the club. My classmate waves to me, and I wave goodbye.

twenty-five

Now for the hyphen years, which do not begin until we have come of age: twenty-one and counting. They imply a perforation, each small dash like a saloon door. They mean to show us how the present swings—the present tears—both ways. And what does love do? Love allows us to swivel.

In my twenty-first year, I shed virginity like a veil. I am lighter, no longer standing guard over phantom treasure.

In my twenty-second year, I leave a man at the altar. I am lighter still, trusting in the power of unspoken vows, the *via negativa* by which both our lives are spared.

In my twenty-third year, I make a new life with a woman. By my twenty-fourth year, I have forgotten how to sleep alone.

And so it is that on the morning of my twenty-fifth birthday, I wake in crescent pose curled around my lover's body. This is our excursion to Sistersville, West Virginia, where we will be mistaken for sisters by everyone we meet. This is a haunted inn—the gift itself—where I will mistake bad plumbing for ghosts in the bathtub. I have always been interested in what becomes of the essence of us—the wick extinguished, but not the rising smoke; the nose of the kite severed, set free from its tail.

A tear: My parents and I are becoming ghosts to each other. They recede to ether in the rearview mirror. Their bodies, a quarter century before, gave rise to mine—as yeast to dough—but there is some essence of my own that transcends them and some essence of theirs that I do not possess or have lost and will never regain. Does it make any sense to say that I mourn the distance spreading like water between us—mourn it without regret?

A swivel: I have gone forth not to multiply but to bond. I have discovered a love electrovalent in its intensity, multivalent in its expression. The phrase *same-sex relationship* never fails to surprise me. How ionic we are, how differently charged! And then to think of the friend whose father once said, "Homosexuality is nothing but vanity, Narcissus gazing at his own reflection in a lover's face." My rebuttal, ten years in the making: *The beloved's body is not a looking glass. The beloved is not a metonym. She stands for nothing but herself.*

A leap back, incredulous: How am I now the age Mrs. Miller was fifteen years ago? I had imagined I would inhabit a womanhood like hers. After all, she taught us the word *paragon*, for a spelling test, and its synonym, *epitome*, to expand our lexicons. Mrs. Miller had embodied these terms for me: the paragon of twenty-five, the epitome of a woman in her middle-twenties.

When I fell in love with her, I fell in love with fulcra.

On her desk, I remember how Mrs. Miller kept a folder labeled MIS-CELLANY, and when I asked what it was for, she said, "For everything that doesn't fit into the other boxes." Perhaps Mrs. Miller had become a woman in the most literal sense. I could hear the hyphen in it: *wo-man*, deriving from or in relation to *man*. The year before we had known her as a first-grade teacher named Miss Baer, but when her prefix changed, she seemed to be, all at once, solidified, her foundation settled. She even moved to a different classroom, a higher grade. Was this how words embedded themselves in the body, like fragments of glass and shell inside a stone? Was marriage or what it signified—*heterosexuality*—something we could see or at least perceive?

And was what I felt at twenty-five even *womanly*, or was it, in fact, *miscellaneous*? I was taking gender studies classes in graduate school. Suddenly, every nevus was presumed to mean something, to reveal a long-dormant truth. Friends were coming out of the woodwork to tell me they had "always known" I was a lesbian. They could "just tell." Should I add it as a prefix to my name? Should I claim it as an ontological category of existence? Could this word explain anything at all about my unique, peculiar, one-of-a-kind embodiment—why, for instance, I could never sit comfortably on my knees?

Then, a woman asked, "Why do you wince when I call you what you are—a woman who loves women? Are you ashamed?"

I shook my head. I was haunted by the sound of the word, not what it sought to convey.

"So, what is it?" she pressed.

"I just don't think I can answer to a name that falls between *leprosy* and *lesion* in the dictionary."

I didn't know her well. She had a ghostly face and dark hair that hid her eyes. "Maybe try a different dictionary," she said. "They're adding new words all the time."

thirty

I turn the big 3-0 standing in the checkout line of a grocery store I no longer frequent in a city where I no longer live. The digital clock switches to midnight as I swipe my debit card. "Your Marlboros, ma'am, and your cash."

I had wanted to smoke, for nostalgia's sake, while passing through our past life in Pittsburgh. This was also, as it happened, Mr. Rogers' neighborhood—a show my love and I both watched as children. The ultimate prolepsis Pittsburgh turned out to be, for we had gone on to inhabit a place inside the television, twenty years after our first glimpse of it on screen.

Is this phenomenon *surreal* or *hyperreal*? I couldn't tell you now. I learned those words in my twenties when my education in theory began. At first, I was attracted to theory because it seemed to lack a body. Theories were *ethereal*, weren't they? A purely cerebral subject, I thought, and I knew I was better, as the saying went, "in theory than in practice."

In Pittsburgh, I had a professor who some referred to as a "theory head." I wanted to be one, too—a theory head but also a gumshoe. As it turned out, this professor rode my bus and lived in my neighborhood. I thought he was smart and intimidating and gay without wanting to presume any correlation among these things. After a low score on my essay, he invited me to meet him for coffee at the Katerbean.

"It turns out I'm not very good at theory," I apologized outright.

"What makes you say that?"

"Your comments on my paper—and the grade."

"Well, any good theory is meant to be the mode of transportation, not the cargo. Do you see what I mean?"

"It's an analogy," I offered sheepishly.

"OK. Let me say this another way: It's as if you're putting too much trust in the theories we've studied." He swallowed a dark shot of espresso in a bright-white cup. "Theory doesn't give you answers to questions. Theory gives you the questions."

And I could see how this was not unlike the way the body could give you a pain, calling your attention to some aspect of yourself you might otherwise overlook or prefer to ignore. Theory was painful like that. It could bruise you, scald you, could even make you pick at your own scabs.

Later, the same professor told me he had learned that many members of the faculty believed he was gay when they hired him. In fact, he was married to a woman. He wondered—and perhaps this wonder needled him the way a theory surely would—if the assumption that he was gay had made him appear a more compelling candidate for the position he now held.

"Do you know why they thought you were gay?" I asked. Why had I been so certain, so insistent that the gay body was marked in some way and that I knew the way? If I could recognize what I had seen or failed to see in him, perhaps I could discern and articulate at last what I had seen or failed to see in myself.

"Well, I got tired of speculating, so I asked around." He was chuckling now. "I found out that most people thought I was gay because I have a woman's middle name!"

Now I am called thirty, which sounds like theory, which reminds me of Cherríe L. Moraga's *theories in the flesh*, which I am teaching to my own students in a gender studies class. I teach with questions, which is the way I have learned to move through the world: What does it mean to say, *the physical realities of our lives* [. . .] *fuse to create a politic born out of necessity?* Moraga insists we do this *by naming our selves and telling our stories in our own words.* By analogy, I might say that language is the consummation of our longing to name at last who we are—to make ourselves known.

In my thirtieth year, my first book is published, my first attempt at naming my self—or selves—of telling my story in my own words. One blurb describes the book as *written from the body,* and when I read this writer's words, I wince at first, the way the word *lesbian* has made me wince for years. I want so much to be praised for my intellect, even as I must know by now that the body was, and is, the ultimate reality to be reckoned with, the site of the truest intelligence, of which and from which I have been writing all along.

Perhaps the reviewer means to suggest I am a theory in the flesh. Aren't we all, in fact—strange constellations of arms and legs, skeletons and cells, somatic questions pulsing to be asked? I write and thank her. Then, I plunge deeper into the white pools of the page.

thirty-five

Every tour of the past culminates in a present, and every past resides in the body, incubated by memory and imagination.

At my age now, my mother was new to motherhood. I cannot remember her then, of course—we had only just met each other. But she used to recount how she had pined for me and how, when I arrived at last—her "miracle baby, against all odds"—she spent her thirty-fifth winter holding and rocking, long hours unmoved from a chair.

Perhaps I am more miscellaneous than my mother. She believed a woman was not truly a woman—could not call herself such—until she became a mother. *What was she before?* But I am always before to my mother, always other, because I have never taken after.

In my thirty-fifth year, my marriage becomes legal in the state where I live. I have been pining for this moment for years and, when it arrives, at last, I bawl like a baby watching tender news stories, the Miami verdict replayed and replayed: "The stay is lifted."

Like my mother perhaps, before she had me or could be certain I would ever be born, I was afraid to admit how much I wanted my marriage. I am still afraid it will be taken away. My love and I have not changed our names the way our mothers did, and yet a name has been changed for us, modified: We are *married women* now.

My father once told me I would never be a woman in his eyes until I married—until he had "given me away." He mentioned nothing about children, but perhaps they were implied. Even now, with all these silver threads in my hair, I suspect my father wouldn't see me as "grown." Even now, with this ring on my hand and this vow in my heart, I suspect my father wouldn't see me.

I do not believe in the two-become-one any more than I believe the two must become three. "Do you have a credo?" an interviewer asks. She wants to know if there is something that cinches my life, that binds together my body of work.

"Recursion is my credo," I say. I touch back, as if to the shore or the wall of a swimming pool. I pivot, then push off again. *Flutter, flutter,* I might have said. *Flip-turn.*

"You're in danger, I fear," an editor notes, "of telling the same stories over and over."

But isn't that what we do? Isn't that what it means to be human? What I had wanted was to plumb them thoroughly, all those porous stories of the past. With only anaphora to guide me, I search them out: *Which ones hold water? Which ones contain seeds?* And if theories are questions, can't credos be, too? *What do we know that we don't yet know we know?*

In my thirty-fifth year, my first book is released in a second printing. It is a not a sequel, as some have wondered, but a renewal, a literary kind of recursion. They are the same words inside but preceded by a new cover. So it is with the body aging—that synonym for growing and changing—but always, some deeper essence abides.

Stripped of descriptors—*woman, lesbian, married*—each body develops its own way of being in the world. Here in the sticky South Florida heat, my body develops an affinity for linen—that ghost of the fabrics, that *there* and *not-there* at once.

"I am my own person," I repeat before falling asleep. "I have made my own family," I smile into the mirror. While climbing mountains on the spin bike, taking pride in the strength of my thighs, I remind myself how unlike my mother I am. I will not fear size. I will not fret curves. Mine is a body in love and in motion, the most honest incarnation I have been.

Then, a twist: the climactic moment of the fragmented narrative. I have written the book and called it "a memoir in fractures." I have mentioned therein my mother's forecast that I am "headed for a fall." *In love*, I hoped. *From grace*, she feared. We are alike in this way, my mother and I: the literal always lost on us with our fondness for figures of speech.

When I slip in a flood on the kitchen floor, my love hears a sound like shattered glass. "Did you drop a bottle?" she calls from the other room. "Are you taking out the recycling?"

It is my leg, both long bones severed above the ankle. I sit on the ground without moving or making a sound. There is no pain, not yet. There is only premonition. I know in an instant how I will spend my thirty-fifth winter: long hours unmoved from a chair.

This is my body broken before me—on the stretcher, in the wheelchair, on the table in the operating room. This is my first visceral and undeniable vulnerability, though I understand that it will not be my last. To fall is inevitable, one way or another. To flourish in spite of fracture is the only choice we have.

Before I go under, I hear some nurses talking in the room. They are laughing and making plans for the weekend. Everything they don't like they call "gay." My body is neither here nor there. They move around me as water glides around rocks. Is it a gay body they see? Is it marked in some way? The word floats across the room like a stray balloon. I try to grasp it with my teeth, but instead I sleep. When I wake, the memory weighs heavy and sour on my tongue.

What to make of this body now, beginning again: its curses and recurses. A friend laments, "When I said 'Break a leg!' at your reading, I meant it as a metaphor!" I flex my foot like the day's greatest accomplishment. I wiggle my toes as an act of divination. When I balance in tree pose and meet my own eyes in the mirror, I see how I am a metaphor, but not only a metaphor.

And when I sink into the bathtub at last, its bubbled caesura, I study the half-moons of the incision sites, their deep purple zippers of scab, the bruise I can only describe as *sui generis*. "A fracture blister," the doctor says. Gravity is never an easy lesson.

This year I am more legs than torso again. I move as if on stilts, an embarrassment on crutches. I begin to memorize what does not come naturally to me: *going slow, taking it easy, sitting still*, as my tibia and fibula do the difficult knitting I could never perform with my hands. May they be prodigious. May I be patient. May my love feel this gratitude rising like steam from my skin.

How Do You Like Them

In the Storybook, there is always a great red apple with a little patch of shine.

Sometimes several apples nestle in a fruit bowl, suggestive of affection. Another sits upright on a teacher's desk, balanced on its awkward apple-buttocks. This one is all business.

Sometimes the apple has a stem, like a cowlick on a little boy's head. Sometimes the stem bears two green leaves, which dangle midair, perfectly symmetrical, an allusion to Dali's mustache.

Sometimes the apple is anthropomorphized, red as a lady's lips, with long eyelashes and a beguiling smile. She seems to want to be bitten or kissed. It is hard to tell which. Perhaps it is always hard to tell which.

Instead of *Goodnight Moon*, I liked to say "Goodnight Apple." If the sun was an orange in the sky, how was the moon not an apple?

In the Storybook, there is always a great red apple, and sometimes a friendly green worm chews its way out from the inside. This is another kind of metamorphosis, different from caterpillars and cocoons.

Call it an apple, the poem begins. *Call this a test or a joke.*

The apple and the worm are friends. Sometimes, the worm wears spectacles and a bow tie. Always, the worm is there to teach the apple something.

My mother called it the "apple of my cheek," that high place under the eye with its little patch of shine.

How Do You Like Them

A black eye is sometimes called "a shiner," or "an apple," according to my father. "Just look at the apple he gave him!" my father exclaims. This is an exciting occasion, though not an especially happy one.

At the Cinema, music swells, lights grow dim, and curtains part, red as apples. When the evil queen appears on screen, I cannot stop screaming. It is a reflex, primal as anything. My father carries me up the long aisle, slung over his shoulder like a sack of fruit.

In the old black-and-white movies we watch on television, a jaunty man may rub an apple on his shirtfront before taking a bite. In these movies, the bite even sounds red.

In the Storybook, God calls David the "apple of His eye." I would rather God had called him the "apple in His sky."

Among things frequently juggled, apples are prominent, along with tennis balls, responsibilities, and bowling pins aflame.

In the Storybook, God makes a small orchard in the middle of a garden. This scene is familiar to me. I have spent hours climbing my friend Joy's apple tree, dangling perfectly in midair, plucking bright fruit from the boughs. Every spring, for the few weeks it flowers, the apple tree turns white as snow.

I ask my mother if Eden is in Washington.

I had a Granny Smith, but we always called her "Grandma." Perhaps this was to distinguish her from the apple, which was also known to be tart.

My other grandma was named after summer. When I bruised my knees, she called the piebald places "apples," then kissed them with her cool, thin lips.

At the Cinema, I puff with pride when Little Orphan Annie recites her long list of dinner wishes: "Did you hear? Did you hear? She asked for Washington apples!"

I ask my mother if I can have a whole apple in my lunchbox, please. The sliced ones turn brown as wilted leaves.

In the Storybook, Eve meets a snake in the garden. He encourages her to eat the apple. He encourages her to learn.

Later, though, Mother puts the apple into Snow White's hand, and then it's poison!

Grandma June cautions that Halloween candy must always be wrapped: "If someone gives you an apple, you take it, you say thank you, and then you run right home. Don't bite it. Give it to your mother."

In the Storybook, the serpent reminds Eve it is important to share. She gives Adam a bite of her apple. They are having a picnic the way I always imagined brothers and sisters do.

"But what happens if I bite it?"

My father tells me one notable difference between men and women is the Adam's apple. Men have an apple lodged in their throats. I have seen it in the game called Operation. Women do not. My father cannot explain this absence, even though the First Man and the First Woman both ate from the same apple tree.

"There could be a razor blade inside."

Later, I learn that women have apples in their throats, too. Though typically smaller and less visible, this protrusion from the larynx protects the vocal cords of men and women alike. Pleased with myself, I boast to my father that I have an Eve's apple. For some reason, he does not look pleased.

I dream my father shoots me with a single arrow. It is an accident, though he is a poor marksman and should not be shooting at all. The arrow does not pierce my heart but lodges deep in my throat instead. *I am not dead,* I marvel, *but I will not speak again.* In the dream, my blood is the color of apples, which is also the color of my mother's dream car. She, like Prince, wants a little red Corvette. This is precisely where the similarities between Prince and my mother end.

I must have been eight years old before I knew apples came in colors other than red.

Have you noticed how the early story problems are all about apples? For instance: *If I pick twelve red apples and you pick nine green apples, how many apples do we have?*

But I thought we weren't supposed to be picking apples at all!

"That's a different story," my father says. This is one of his favorite things to say.

Eve has five more apples than Adam. Adam has nine apples. How many apples does Eve have? It is hard to think of *fourteen* at a time like this, knowing they are naked and sunburned and eventually going to die.

When I feel sick as a child, my mother gives me applesauce. In winter, she warms it up and adds cinnamon. In summer, she serves it cold.

Sometimes I have a strong desire to be sick in the middle of winter so I can eat warm applesauce dusted with cinnamon.

"An apple a day keeps the doctor away," Grandma June was fond of saying. Grandma Smith, who was not fond of apples or anything else, goes into the hospital and never comes out.

At one time, we discussed a family vacation to New York City, sometimes known as the Big Apple. In the end, my parents decided it was too dangerous and expensive. We traveled to Portland, Oregon, instead, which is known as the City of Roses.

If gas costs $.89 per gallon, and the destination city is 2,404 miles away, how much will it cost to make the trip? What if the destination city is only 173 miles away?

My father chuckled. "That's like comparing apples and oranges"—as if he invented the phrase.

Despite my years of pleading, my mother never puts a whole apple in my lunchbox. She says it is "unladylike" for a girl to eat an apple that way.

In the Storybook, Trixie Belden lives on Crabapple Farm. I don't know what a crabapple is, but I know I want to live with Trixie Belden in a houseboat on Puget Sound.

Speculative questions prove infinitely more appealing than those with fixed answers: *When Julie and Trixie make their first apple-based dessert, should it be a crumble or a cobbler or a pie?* And *how many apples will these two enterprising sleuths and inseparable friends require?* And *will they be too shy to kiss in a windstorm and pluck apple petals from each other's hair?*

How Do You Like Them

I like to jump rope to the names of apples. Two syllables are best: Fu-ji. Brae-burn. Ga-la. Pink Crisp.

In one Storybook, the man-gardener called Adam apprentices himself to a master orchardist called God, who bellows at him from inside a cloud. In another Storybook, the man-gardener called Johnny apprentices himself to a master orchardist called Mr. Crawford, who speaks to him face-to-face. The first orchard is in Eden. The second orchard is in Ohio.

My mother teaches me how to make an apple cake from her secret recipe. The cake is ugly to look at but tastes better than all the pretty desserts I've ever had. Apple cake also puts carrot cake to shame.

In one Storybook, Johnny Chapman is such a good gardener and grower of apples that his name is changed to Johnny Appleseed. I ask my father if Adam from the other Storybook has a last name. He says "No," then "I don't know," then "Maybe Child-of-God?"

It is harder to jump rope to Jon-a-gold, Pa-ci-fic Rose, and Pau-la Red, though I do decide to write a story about a woman named Paula Red who always carries a lucky apple in her purse and solves mysteries that stump the police. She bears a certain resemblance to Carmen Sandiego.

Before piano lessons, I sit at Mr. Van Lierop's brand-new computer and answer questions about B-flat and grace notes and four-four time. He has taught me how to turn the computer on and insert the floppy disk that contains the questions. There are many levels, so mastery seems unlikely. Sometimes the question times out because I spend too long gazing at the rainbow-colored apple perched seductively above the keyboard. Someone has already taken a bite.

Whenever I see a word and the thing it signifies placed side by side, I feel a surge of satisfaction. My pulse quickens in my wrist. My toes wiggle in my shoes. My breath catches in my throat like a scarf in a screen door. In this case, the image of an apple paired with the word *apple* is more thrilling than I can ever hope to explain.

Meanwhile, my class is the only class in the whole building with a computer, so all day long little children traipse in and out, placing a finger over their lips as the teacher taught them, waiting in line for their turn to identify words or numbers on the screen. Their presence makes us feel older, more important. They are dwarves, and we are Snow White, every last one of us.

Despite pervasive connotations of sin, temptation, and forbidden truth, the Apple remains a mandatory site of learning all my youth.

Once upon a time, after Adam but before the present day, there was a very smart man named Isaac Newton who liked to sit in his garden and think. He was not the same Newton of the fig empire. If he were, the little cakes would have been stuffed with jellied apples, no doubt.

Mr. Newton thought about a lot of things, but he was especially interested in notions of motion. He was, after all, a scientist. One day, while sitting in the shade of an apple tree, Mr. Newton had an epiphany. The epiphany coincided with an apple dropping from the tree, and, in some versions, conking Mr. Newton on his highly sensitive head. At that moment, Mr. Newton realized that the apple fell to the earth, gaining speed as it fell, because an invisible force acted upon it. He did not call this force *God*. He called it *gravity*, and he saw that it was good. Mr. Newton imagined the apple tree growing taller and taller, and still, apples would plummet to earth every time they were roused by wind.

If gravity could act upon even the tallest tree, even the Tree of Life, say, or the Tree of Knowledge of Good and Evil, could gravity not also reach the moon, the sky's greatest known apple? Might gravity even explain the moon's faithful orbit of the earth? Mr. Newton wrote down his theory and shared it with other scientists, who agreed that the apple and its gravity were good.

My father is also fond of saying, "A rotten apple spoils the whole barrel"— as if he invented the phrase. In my future life, I will wonder if I am the rotten fruit to which my father refers.

At least half the time, my mother says "sour apples" instead of "sour grapes." She becomes more irate when I attempt to correct her. In my future life, I will wonder if I am the sour fruit to which my mother refers.

Both parents scold me for bruising bananas when unloading the grocery bags. When a banana is bruised, the damage is obvious, each brown patch set in sharp contrast to the yellow peel. But apples are sometimes bruised in ways that are not obvious until you bite them. There is often an unexpected sweetness to the bruise.

Once upon a time, after Adam but before the present day, Robert Frost picked apples from the trees in his garden. After he had picked *ten thousand*

thousand of them, which may have been hyperbole to convey his inundation, Mr. Frost became weary and fell asleep, though he continued to dream of apples. He was, after all, a writer. In his dream: *Magnified apples appear and disappear, Stem end and blossom end, And every fleck of russet showing clear.* Mr. Frost could not escape the apples, which became a metaphor for other responsibilities he had grown weary of juggling. He illustrated the paradox best this way: *For I have had too much Of apple-picking: I am overtired Of the great harvest I myself desired.* Frost's was a recognizable feeling, like eating too much ice cream and getting a bellyache, or wanting to stay home alone and then feeling afraid and longing for your parents' return. My teachers told me Frost was contemplating his own death, the loss of his will to live, but I never believed them. Wasn't every day shiny and new, bright as a Red Delicious? Weren't some days even covered in caramel?

My friend April's father can eat a whole apple, including the stem, seeds, and core. In this way, he resembles a horse I met once on a field trip. Nothing is wasted on him.

I discover two people eating apples together in the same room at the same time can be very pleasant. If only one person is eating an apple, the feelings that arise in the other may range from mild annoyance to homicidal rage.

My friend April and I take a quiz in *Seventeen* magazine to determine our body types. Options include Apple, Pear, Ruler, and Hourglass. "Two are food, and two are devices of measurement," I muse. According to the article, neither one of us is an apple. April, however, is easily recognizable as a pear. "I like pears," she says, accepting her fruit-fate. But even when I use the tape measure *for best results*, my body shape remains *inconclusive.*

My mother is fond of saying, "The apple doesn't fall far from the tree." This phrase has many meanings, but in context, it suggests that I, like my mother-tree, am not a natural beauty. Examples of natural beauties, according to my mother, include movie stars like Audrey Hepburn and Gwyneth Paltrow. It is hard to ascertain which shape each actress embodies, but I notice the adjective most frequently used to describe them is *willowy*, which leads us back to trees. This seems like a linguistic dead end to me. When I say "I'm stumped," it becomes a pun.

My friend April decides that Hepburn and Paltrow are rulers. "How can you tell?" April suggests *ruler* has a second meaning beyond its shape, like *ruler of male attention* or *ruler of the social scene.*

Later, I learn that Audrey Hepburn ate a dish of tart green apples every night for dessert. I wonder if this was pure coincidence or part of a carefully controlled health and beauty regimen.

Grandma June was fond of saying, "An apple a day keeps the doctor away." But what kind of doctor did she actually mean—a specialist in bariatrics?

Later, I learn that Gwyneth Paltrow named her firstborn Apple. Much later, I learn that mother and preteen daughter undergo expensive facials performed by a beauty therapist in Hollywood. I consider their picture in a magazine: Apple resembles her mother, just as I resemble mine.

In high school, I write a poem about punctuation. In it, I declare: *The asterisk is the apple of the lexical world.* Sister Mary Annette slashes through words until the paper resembles my own pale arms after a day in the thicket picking blackberries. At the bottom of the page, a note: *I have no idea what you're talking about! Poems must at least make sense.*

Later, I read Pablo Neruda in a library book: *Carnal apple, Woman filled, burning moon, dark smell of seaweed, crush of mud and light, what secret knowledge is clasped between your pillars?*

Still later, I read Jennifer Oakes in a literary journal: *It would take fire or breaking glass to tell them the poppy, the apple, and the vein.*

And still, later, I hear Katerina Stoykova-Klemer read her poem, "The Apple Who Wanted to Become a Pinecone" at a festival in Owensboro, Kentucky: *I can see why a pinecone would wish to be an apple, but it is less obvious why an apple would want to be a pinecone.*

It is obvious enough to me. My own desires move back and forth across furrows, hedgerows, little flags in the soil. Pinecones sometimes fall close to the tree, while apples sometimes fall far, and vice versa. No matter what I do, or what I refrain from doing, there is always a *vice* and a *versa*. There is always Fiona Apple singing a sad, sexy song on the scratched CD.

I decide I am both the apple and the pinecone in the poem, soft flesh and bristled body, deciduous and coniferous at once. I decide Sister Mary Annette is wrong.

At one time, I used a Blackberry as my electronic device, enamored by its tablet shape and tiny keypad. But there was another reason. I loved that the product name also called to mind a treasured poem: *Such tenderness, those afternoons and evenings, saying blackberry, blackberry, blackberry.* If apple was the fabled fruit of the fall, perhaps blackberry was the fruit of a sweeter time, a different story—something about redemption or the promise of it. Like most treasures, my Blackberry did not last.

In the hotel lobby, I spy a platter of impossibly ripe apples, more pleasing than any bouquet of roses or bottle of Beaujolais. When the concierge sees me eyeing them, he insists, "Take one. They're complimentary." I blush. "Would you mind if I took all of them?" His brow sags until I show him my camera. It is also an Apple. We both laugh.

Now I'm thinking of a game from childhood. "Hi-ho-something? Do you remember?" I ask my beloved. "Cherry-o," she says. "No, I think it's *cheerio*, like the British say in greeting or parting or making a toast." "But they're cherries," she insists. "The whole game was about picking cherries from a tree." I'm certain they were apples. We look it up. They were cherries. "All those years I remembered it wrong. I thought I was picking apples!" "Maybe you were," she laughs.

I remember my first candy apple at the circus. My mother walks in to find me squatting on the counter, all the apples from the crisper laid out in a row. I am covering them with peanut butter and colored sprinkles, which is how I assume you turn an apple into candy.

Somewhere I am pleading in the checkout line for Grandma June to buy me Aplets & Cotlets. She always does. We pile the sugary delicacies on a saucer between us, then gorge until our lips are powdered white, our fingers sticky with the hybrid treat—apples, apricots, and walnuts.

Somewhere Elliott the Dragon is roasting apples on the flame of his own breath, then tossing one—still too hot to eat—to the boy named Pete, whose hair is the same color as that flame. Pete always blows on the apple, takes a bite, and then begins to sing. Here is an only child who is never lonely, a boy with an apple-roasting dragon for a friend. I rewind and watch them, over and over again.

Though I never learn to make applesauce, I learn to make apple-centos instead:

> *How do you like them apples I keep hearing from the cellar bin,*
> *The rumbling sound; let a loose apple teach me how to spin.*
> *Welcome the ripe, the sweet, the sour, even wasps at work*

in the soft flesh. The apple apologizes
for those whose hearts bear too much zest.
We could grow apples here . . . Apples?
Red apples hearty in the trees, golden apples
in sheer skin. Their weight breaks branches,
the ground rolls with them: white apples
and the taste of stone.

Once, I played the evil queen in a school play, brandishing a plastic poison apple. Although I cried when the teacher first assigned me the part, I soon learned that villains have better lines.

Once, a student who worked the lunch rush at Whole Foods brought me an apple, placed it lovingly on my desk. "This is a Macintosh," she told me. "They're the very best."

Once, in an interview, Gwyneth Paltrow explained that she loved the idea of calling her baby her little pomme, which is French for *apple*. Depending how you say it, the French for apple also sounds like *poem*.

In one Storybook, Johnny Appleseed never marries or has any children of his own. He spends his life scattering apple seeds, which grow into magnificent orchards and secure his legacy.

One day, when I am grown, I live in Ohio for a while, where I run through apple orchards in autumn with the woman I love. We drink cider made fresh from those trees and sold in jugs from the back of pickup trucks piebald as any Pink Lady. In that life, I think of Johnny Appleseed, wondering if he was gay like me, happy like me, and if he too dreamed of leaving Ohio.

In another Storybook, Adam Child-of-God marries Eve Child-of-God, who shares his last name and is made from his own rib. I find this fact instinctively distasteful, though no one else in Vacation Bible School seems to mind. The Children-of-God are evicted from their botanical home, after which they run a failed landscaping business on the outskirts of Eden. Eve is cursed with terrible menstrual cramps, long before Pamprin is invented. Eventually, she and her husband have two sons, one of whom grows up and kills the other. It is probably good they are the first people because they would have trouble finding a bright spot to highlight in their family Christmas card.

One day, when I am grown, I pack up that Storybook with the gold-gilt pages, the red velvet bookmark, and the smooth vellum cover. I finally put it away. Then, I marry the woman I love in my home state of Washington, a small ceremony without ceremony by the sea. Sometimes, I still think of those stories, of the ways they are sewn into my skin like names into camp clothes, but I never reopen that volume.

Nine Innings

1.

My father used to tell me I took after him. He said this while praising my "zest for life," pleased that I was "slow to anger and quick to joy." What he didn't say, what he always stopped short of saying, was this: *I'm so thankful you take after me and not your mother.*

It's June 2003, and I haven't seen my father since Christmas. I call him from a pay phone on East Marginal Way, offer to take him to lunch.

"Are you alone?" he hedges.

"Angie is with me," I say. And I know in my heart that Angie will always be with me. I think my father knows, too.

"Well, this is . . . *unexpected.* It's a busy day, and I only take half an hour for lunch, not to mention the fact that your mother is—"

"It's you I wanted to see, Dad. Tell me where you like to eat around here, and we'll meet you there in twenty minutes."

Angie isn't sure she should join us for lunch at Best Café and Teriyaki. We have tried this once before, last November—a sit-down meal with my parents on Alki Beach—the two of us on one side of the table, the two of them on the other. But before we made it inside the restaurant, my mother ranted at us on the sidewalk, stopping traffic with her rage.

"She won't be there," I promise. "And it's important for my father to see us together, to know that we're not hiding, that he can't imagine you away."

My father, a blue-eyed man with a matching blue jacket, tries to smile as he passes through the plate glass door. I rise to greet him and watch the way he winces, as if it hurts to look at me now. He nods at Angie and extends a tepid hand.

"Well, what a nice surprise," he sighs. This is his best salesman's speak, and still, I do not believe him. The waitress knows my father, expedites his glass of iced tea with several sugar packets.

"Good afternoon, Mr. Bill. How lucky you are to be dining with two young ladies!"

"This is my daughter." He gestures toward me, and I catch a glimpse of his former pride. *This daughter, the one who takes after him.* "She's just graduated from a Master's program at Western Washington University." Now he studies the menu he knows by heart. "And this is her friend from school."

"Very nice, very nice," the waitress nods, a pencil stashed in her shiny black hair. "I'll give you all a minute to decide."

A minute is not going to be long enough for this decision, though. It has been ten months since I told my parents I love a woman—not some anonymous girl or fleeting crush, but this flesh-and-blood woman beside me, this beloved my father has reduced to a friend.

"Dad, I'm leaving," I say.

"Don't be silly. We haven't even ordered yet."

"No. I mean—Angie and I are moving out of state. I've been accepted to some graduate programs back East, and . . . "

"What are you talking about? You've just finished graduate school."

"Yes, but I'm not done. Really, in the whole scheme of things, I'm just getting started. And Angie is coming with me because we're just getting started, too."

I should say here: I know my father loves me. I have never doubted his love for his only child, his longed-for, late-in-life daughter. But facing him now across this sticky table, struggling to meet and hold his eyes, I understand that I am the battle my father is losing. Should he ever see me again, it will be as a monument—some great and glowing marker of his defeat.

"So this is goodbye then?" His voice falls low and flat. The fizz is gone.

"It doesn't have to be goodbye in some permanent way, but what happens next depends on you."

"I don't see that you've left me any choice," he replies.

"All I want is for you to acknowledge who Angie is to me, who we are to each other. We're not roommates. We're not study buddies. We're not *pals*."

The waitress returns, but my father waves her brusquely away. This is unlike him, the man who is slow to anger and quick to joy.

"Can't we just have lunch?" he pleads. "We don't have to talk about any of this . . . *unpleasantness* now." He sounds more like himself again.

Angie is gazing out the window at bird shit on gravel. The view leaves something to be desired. My father is holding the laminate page in his hands like the Gospel according to John. He wishes I had read the Bible more. Behind my knees, sweat is pooling and pooling, two cups that are soon to spill. I can't decide if I am a hostage about to break free, or if my father is the hostage I am going to take with me. The only word I can think of is *siege*.

"You really should have invited your mother to this lunch," he says, unraveling the paper napkin and placing it in his lap. "She misses you, and it isn't right to exclude her."

We all look over at the waitress now, only to find it isn't her. Two men from my father's work loom near our table, grinning. "Are we interrupting something, Bill?"

"Tom, Mike—no, no, not at all." The bubbles return to his voice, the levity, the laughter. He stands up and shakes both their hands firmly. "Let me introduce my daughter, Julie."

"Oh, your father just can't shut up about you. It's Julie-this and Julie-that all day long. I'm beginning to think you're Superwoman or something."

This, of course, will change. History is always written from the victor's point of view.

"Now the only thing he has to worry about is when you're going to meet your Superman!"

I look at my father and then at the men, all of them clean-shaven, neatly pressed: their khaki slacks with deep pleats, their polo shirts with pocket logos. Each hairy hand with its thick gold band.

"This is Angie," I say. "She's my—"

"*Friend* from school," my father intercedes. "They're classmates up at Western Washington. Just passing through and thought they'd give me a call."

He thumps the table with his knuckles, and all the ice leaps to the top of his glass.

2.

It happens through the mail, too: this writing over, this striking through.

My mother bemoans the price of postage, yet still her letters arrive, overstuffed as ever and Scotch-taped to oblivion. The script is tidy, precise—so unlike mine. The "P"s in Pittsburgh and Pennsylvania perform a full salute. The seals on her envelopes are girls in silhouette. Think Holly Hobbie and her famous bonnet.

This is the mother I do not take after, she who is quick to anger and slow to joy, whose passion is for appearances. She knows things, this mother, about flower arranging and piano playing, about setting a nice table and saying a fine grace. She has never set foot outside the house without rouge on her cheeks and paint on her lips. Her chandelier glitters even in the dark.

And make no mistake: This mother knows me, or so she believes. Her expertise extends to my desires, spoken or unspoken, my greatest wishes and fears. She has read every novel ever written by Danielle Steel, which surely counts for something. In other words, she is prodigious and undeterred where other people's happiness is concerned.

If a letter came from my mother now, here is what it might say:

Dear Julie,

I'm thinking of you as always and praying you know how much we love you. It must be hard to be so far away from home. If you were here, I would make you hot cocoa and put clean sheets on your bed, and then we could all relax together as a family.

You may or may not know that Danielle Steel has written a memoir about the suicide of her son Nick. Of this book, Danielle writes, "I want to share the story, and the pain, the courage, the love, and what I learned in living through it. I want Nick's life to be not only a tender memory for us, but a gift to others . . . My hope is that someone will be able to use what we learned, and save a life with it."

Please put aside your snide opinions about her fiction. I believe this book was put into my hands so that I could learn from what Danielle Steel learned about her son and ultimately save the life of my daughter with that knowledge.

Julie, listen to me very closely. You are <u>not</u> gay. You do <u>not</u> hate your parents. You are suffering from manic depression, just as Nick was. This untreated condition has caused you to lash out at us, to become confused about your true affections and where your real loyalties lie. As is so often the case, manic depression has made you think you are gay when really you are just imbalanced. There are people who can help you—specialists who can regulate your hormones and give you a new lease on life.

Please consult a doctor as soon as possible. You might mention this letter or Danielle Steel's book, His Bright Light. *You have a bright light inside you, too, Julie, but no one can see it right now because of your acute mental illness. We will forgive you for everything you have done if you will act now in your own best interest. No grudges and no reprisals, I promise.*

Love,
Mom

3.

Everyone looks shifty in the doctor's waiting room, including me. We rummage through magazines, feign interest in talk-show TV, but our eyes keep wandering to the counter, the list, the next person to be summoned to the secret room. I suppose we are all hiding something we won't reveal until we've stripped down to our skivvies. Then, shivering in a paper gown, we'll wonder why honesty proves so much harder without our clothes on.

I'm twenty-five. This is the first doctor's appointment I've ever made on my own. I'm scared, but I'm here because I read an article that scared me more. Lesbians, studies have shown, are the social group most likely to neglect their health by opting out of annual exams and other forms of preventive care. One theory to explain these findings surmised that lesbians have internalized the message that their lives are not as valuable as others, leading to a lowered sense of self-worth.

This is important to say: Being gay never made me hate myself. If there was a god, I wasn't worried about him hating me either. I lived as a secular humanist by day and a hopeless romantic by night. I believed in following my heart and being true to mine own self, even when that self surprised me. In other words, when I realized I was gay, I wanted to be honest about that fact from the very first day of revelation. For years, I had tried to be out about my life with everyone I knew and everyone I met. The biggest surprise was how frequently I found myself pushed back in.

"You've left a lot of these questions blank," the nurse observes. She is young and matter-of-fact, and I am mesmerized by the blinding chunk of cutlery jutting forth from her left hand.

"They didn't seem applicable," I reply.

"Well, you're either single or married. Let's start there." *Was it the tip of an iceberg?* I marveled. *Could that ring have sunk the Titanic?*

"I'm not single," I say, "and I'm not married. I live with my partner of three years."

"*Single,*" she says, her loud pen-scratch revising my story. "And are you trying to get pregnant?"

Her ring flashes at me like the bright lights they use to interrogate suspects in overwrought television dramas. "You marked that you *are* sexually active but that you *aren't* using birth control?"

"Lesbianism is my birth control," I say, feeling clever all of a sudden, and dangerously smug.

"I see." She doesn't check any more boxes and leaves the room without looking up.

Dr. Berman is a small, efficient woman who rarely smiles and likely inspired the creation of the color taupe. Her skirt is taupe, her shoes are taupe, even her skin is taupe. Since I don't know her first name, I christen her *Diane Taupe Berman* in my mind—*Diane T. Berman* to fit on the shingle.

We shake hands and pretend that my thinly covered nakedness is normal. Once my feet are in the stirrups, my body tilted back at its most vulnerable angle, she asks me: "Were you ever heterosexual?" *Not quite the icebreaker I had imagined.*

"I'm gay," I say. "My partner is a woman."

"Exclusively?" She seems surprised, as if woman cannot live by the love of woman alone.

"Yes, *exclusively.*"

"And you were always with women, never with men?" she clarifies.

"A long time ago I was with a man. I've been to the gynecologist since. I used protection."

Dr. Berman isn't convinced. Perhaps she thinks *this* is the something I'm hiding: my part-time lesbianism, my flimsy commitment to the life I have chosen.

"Men are part of my past, but Angie is my present—and my future." I like the way these words feel on my tongue, sinewy and certain.

Later, I catch a glimpse of my file, the manila folded back just so. "BI-SEXUAL" is written in the margin. The tidy, precise script isn't mine.

4.

In Pittsburgh, I attend one university and work for another.

At school, I have earned a reputation as The Angry Lesbian. It has even been suggested to me that I was only admitted to the program as "diversity." And I was waitlisted after all, so perhaps some more desirable "diversity" turned down the spot in order to make room for me, The Angry Lesbian.

Right now I'm experimenting with my inheritance—which traits are malleable and which are not. For a while, I allow myself to be both my mother's and my father's child—quick to anger *and* quick to joy.

At work, I play The Joyful Lesbian—more Ellen DeGeneres than Valerie Solanas. This version of myself, despite the desire to be edgy and outspoken, feels most authentic to me. I decide to keep her.

There are two bosses at my job. One is a gay woman who has not yet come out of the closet. Let's call her Marsha. The other is a straight man who impersonates a gay man at Costco. Let's call him George.

This is important to say: I am valued and affirmed and genuinely loved,

I think, by both my bosses. They know Angie. They have never downgraded her from "partner" to "friend." They have never treated me as if I were "single," and by extension, fickle, uncommitted. I have no right to feel slighted by their personal choices, and yet—

Every time Marsha does not divulge that she has a partner waiting at home, a woman who has shared her life for more than a decade, I think it again: *Siege.* The word drones in my head, pulses through my veins. I am easier to shoot down when I am The Only One. I feel less invincible in my falsely thick skin. *Let's burn our draft cards, not our gay cards!* I want to chant. I'm not hiding, but I'm protecting someone who is. I'd court-martial myself if I could.

Then, I mobilize the academic part of my mind. I ask myself: How does Marsha's resistance to coming out justify your own sense of being hemmed in, pinned to the periphery of the Mainstream Map, the Settled Territories?

There is no rational answer. I hate it here, alone in the outfield. *Let me out. Let me in.* Does anyone ever win a war like this, where half the people call it a sin and the other half aren't sure what exactly they're fighting for?

"Costco is so progressive," George says. "They recognize marriages *and* domestic partnerships." He is single. His neighbor is, too. They are two men who date women while sharing the cost of a single membership for their make-believe, same-sex household.

"Do you have to go to the store together?" I ask, as if this has nothing to do with me—and perhaps it doesn't.

"No, that's the beauty of it. We're registered as domestic partners, but we each have a card, so we can do our shopping together or separately, and no one is the wiser."

I am no wiser, anyway. It's 2006, then 2007. My parents have told their friends I'm married to a surgeon now and living in New England. If asked, they would like me to please corroborate this story.

How can I say their blatant lie about my life obscures me in the same way as Marsha's self-closeting does? Perhaps I am obscured differently? And how can I say that George's Costco card diminishes me and lives like mine when he and his neighbor are actually making domestic partnerships more visible with their lie?

Straight people play gay people on TV all the time. Didn't *Will & Grace* win seven GLAAD awards?

Marsha has a commitment ceremony one weekend. I am the only friend from work who is invited, and it goes without saying that I shouldn't broadcast the news when I return to the office on Monday. Angie and I both wear dresses with sandals, given the heat. The usher sizes us up, then escorts us to the Straight Table. "Are you sisters?" someone asks.

We continue to buy our groceries at the Giant Eagle, where no membership is required.

5.

"We had a lesbian couple here once before, but it didn't work out so well . . . "

This is Vic Peacock, the woodworking teacher, telling me what I wish I had known six months before. "The folks at the Meeting just weren't ready for it, and the fight to keep those two lady teachers—they were really good at their jobs, I'll give 'em that—led to the split between the church and the school."

Angie and I were vaguely aware of the rumor that "ideological differences" caused the Stillwater Meeting House to separate formally from Olney Friends School in 2001. But six years later, when we signed on to work for the school, we had no idea we were the new "test case," the Better Luck This Time lesbian faculty members.

The married couples are given rent-free houses on the property. We are offered two rent-free apartments in the girls' dorm. "You can arrange them any way you like," Mary Ellen tells us cheerfully. "For instance, one can be for your sleeping quarters, the other for your offices."

"No," we say, firm on this point.

"But you'll have more space with this configuration," she coaxes, pointing to both doors like a deluxe showcase on *The Price Is Right*. "It isn't about appearances."

My mother has taught me otherwise. She believed everything was about appearances—and perhaps, I'm learning, she was right.

I wanted our lives to showcase our truth and not a story someone else has told about us.

"We don't keep two residences," Angie explains. "We share one."

Soon, a social director named Cleda comes around to take our pictures. I am in my classroom, arranging desks. Angie is in the library, cataloging books. We pause and smile for the camera. Neither of us thinks anything of it until the students begin to arrive. Many are coming from out of state and many more from out of the country. *What will boarding school be like?* they wonder in many languages. Then, they crowd close together by the welcome wall, inspect the faculty's varied faces.

"Which one are you?" the Dean of Students asks as we pass each other on the stairs. When I don't respond, he prompts me: "The teacher or the librarian?"

"I'm Julie," I say, extending a tepid hand.

"Micah," he smiles and takes it.

The students disperse for a soccer game on the lawn, but I linger a while before the welcome wall, looking at the faces of the rest of the staff and their families.

There is Thea with her husband Larry, their children perched in the tree behind them. Gavin wears overalls and a denim cap, which make him look like a train conductor from a storybook. Ellie has woven a crown of black-eyed Susans for her hair. There are Shelley and Joel on their front stoop, the sunset framing their faces; Plume, their Husky with the grand white tail, stretches out at their feet and yawns. I see how their names are joined with an ampersand. I see how their pictures tell a family story.

On one corner of the board, I find myself; a yardstick away, I find Angie. We are alone, apart, sans ampersand. *Single* and *straight*, by all visible accounts. Both new hires, perhaps we haven't even met each other yet. Perhaps we are strangers. We appear as all the other new faculty, fresh from college or graduate school, that mix of excitement and nerves.

Surely, we have come to this place unattached, sweating in our dresses and sandals. Surely, we sleep on twin mattresses in our small apartments with their half-baths and kitchenettes. Surely, we have read the policy: *All overnight guests shall stay in the guest house. No sharing of rooms by unmarried members of the community will be tolerated.*

I reach up and tear our pictures down.

6.

Kentucky won't be like Ohio, we promise ourselves. We resolve to put all our paperwork in order before one of us is rushed to the ER with a fever, a cyst, a kidney stone, before the other is left trying to prove she is not just some *coworker*, some *well-meaning acquaintance*.

"She *is* my home! She *is* my family!" I find myself crying before the lights go dim, and my breath lodges deep in my chest.

It's 2009, a rainy Saturday morning in the Louisville Highlands. We walk into our bank. We remind the teller what we've read online: *Customers with a valid checking or savings account are entitled to free notary services.*

"Our notary is actually our manager," the teller replies. "If you'll just have a seat at that desk, I'll ask him to come over."

Angie and I sit down on the plush maroon chairs, and soon a middle-aged man wearing a tie beneath his sweater vest faces us and asks, "How may I help you?"

We have brought our checkbook with our names imprinted and joined by an ampersand. We lay out our debit cards side by side, in case he needs to see these, too. "We're National City customers, and we'd like to have some paperwork notarized."

"What kind of paperwork?" he asks, slipping on his glasses.

"Power of attorney, health power of attorney, living wills." The documents were drawn up for us by an LGBT legal organization based in West Virginia. None of the local lawyers I contacted ever returned my calls.

"I see." He removes his glasses as quickly as he put them on. "I'm afraid you're going to have to take this paperwork elsewhere."

"If there's a service charge," Angie volunteers, "we'd be happy to pay it. We'd just like to have these notarized today."

"It isn't about payment," the manager replies, rising so we are eye level with the pleats of his pants, his hands lodged in his pockets. "I'm just not comfortable notarizing this kind of paperwork."

"But it says on the website that the bank notarizes documents for all its customers. I imagine wills and power of attorney forms are very common."

"They are." He is still facing us, but his body has turned toward the door. "I'm not *personally* comfortable notarizing these documents for persons . . . such as yourselves."

In the moment that follows, I experience a glittering epiphany. I know now how a person, any person, even one such as myself, could rant on the sidewalk, could stop traffic with her rage.

7.

Often when I feel discouraged, I pick a date at random—sometimes a whole year—and I say to myself, "*This* is the future. Just wait until we get *here*." I like to have something to circle in red on the calendar, a visual reminder that time marches forward, not back.

In 2010, I told myself everything would be different. I told myself other things, too. "Louisville is the largest and most liberal city in Kentucky." I think it's true. In spite of everything, I still want to believe it's true.

We've been invited to a dinner party by a liberal Louisvillian and his family. We arrive with wine, bright smiles, high expectations. Our status as a couple is widely known, comfortably acknowledged. A crucible of home-made guacamole beckons from the table. The lighting is soft, and the voices are warm. We feel at ease in this man's home.

The liberal Louisvillian has a daughter. She's seventeen and working on a high school project. Halfway through the hors d'oeuvres she appears frazzled in the doorway. She isn't sure about the order of her poems, and she has to get to the copy store before they close.

"There's a twenty-four-hour Kinko's at the Douglass Loop," I offer. "You have time."

"Julie!" Now the liberal Louisvillian beams at me. "Honey, this is Julie. She's a PhD student at the University. She teaches undergraduates, and her specialty is poetry."

His daughter sighs and pulls her hair back with a scrunchie. Even the future contains these remnants from the past. "Can you help me, please?"

Before I know it, I am reading assignment guidelines and making suggestions about fonts and bindings. She tells me she knows she shouldn't have waited till the last minute. She tells me she has a lot on her mind. It isn't fair the way high school graduation gets overshadowed by all these tests and applications for college.

Her father, lingering nearby, sips a tumbler of bourbon and chats with Angie. "Julie might be able to give you some advice about those applications," he tells his daughter. "Maybe even write you a letter of recommendation."

This is important to say: I don't mind helping a young student I've never met before. In fact, I enjoy it. I am coming into a fuller sense of my vocation, and I like that I can be called upon to share what I know—what I love—with others. My "zest for life," as my father once called it, my zest for poetry and literature at large.

Later, we gather in the living room to hear the daughter play piano. She is self-conscious and proud of herself at the same time, a feeling I know well. She wants to get the song over with as soon as possible, but she also wants to give an encore performance where all the guests at her father's party applaud and beg for more. Afterward, Angie and I commend her talents and wish her well in the coming year.

"It was really great to meet you," she says and shakes my hand so I'll know she means it. "How do you know my dad again?"

The liberal Louisvillian intercedes. "I work with her friend Angie. This is Angie, in case you haven't met. And if you need to get in touch with Julie again, I'm sure Angie will know how to reach her."

Our faces falling now, our hopes besieged. Which is to say: This is the way light fizzles out of a tunnel; this is the way wind passes out of a sail.

8.

All these years I have been writing a book about outings, what it means to come out into the open of the world. Not that the world is always open, but we pry at its fingers and press into its palms. We make ourselves as visible and indelible as we can.

Put another way: not every outing is a picnic; not every outing is a ball game.

But then this happens: the longed-for outing, the dream realized. My first book is published. A transmutation occurs from "writer" to "author." I occupy my subject position in a more public way. Not just an "author" even, but an "LGBT author."

And then this happens: the ultimate outing, the never-even-dared-to-dream. My book wins a prize for LGBT Literature. The gold seal on each book jacket proclaims, "Winner of the Lambda Literary Award for Lesbian Memoir."

There is no going back now, I think, and take my first deep breath in a decade. This book about outings has relieved me of the responsibility for outing myself. People will *know* now, unequivocally. A small mission accomplished. A truce at last.

~

At the university where I learn and teach, a fellow graduate student approaches me at the copy machine. Let's call her Genevieve. Instead of college courses, Genevieve teaches full-time at a local high school. She's interested in bringing "living authors" into her classroom. I am delighted to be considered one of those.

"There's just one thing, though," she tells me, and I recognize the way her words lean on little kickstands, unable to support themselves. "Assumption is a *Catholic* school, and the administration doesn't officially *condone* . . . homosexuality. So if you were to come to my classroom to read from your book and talk to students about it, you wouldn't actually be able to say anything . . . *gay*. You're a really great writer, and I'd love to have you there, but I can't be doing anything that's going to jeopardize my job. I'd like to say I'm willing to put it all on the line for you, but that's just not the reality of my financial situation. There's probably some way we can highlight all your strengths as a personal essayist without—"

"Getting too personal about it?" I'm being sarcastic of course, but no one ever expects sarcasm from me. I think it's the dimples.

"Yes," she says, clapping her hands. "Exactly!"

~

Nine Innings

August 5, 2011

Hi Genevieve,

I just wanted to say thanks for thinking of me regarding the guest author visit at Assumption. It would be great if it worked out, as I genuinely enjoy working with students, and your class that features the personal essay seems so promising. I wish more people taught the personal essay—and long before students arrive at college.

At the same time, though, I'd just as soon not do it if there is going to be any kind of weirdness surrounding my visit or any potentially negative repercussions for you. When I said I wouldn't bring anything "explicit" into your classroom, I meant I wouldn't read an explicit sex scene. That isn't because I think there's anything wrong with sex scenes, but only because it's a matter of audience. I wouldn't read an explicit sex scene to high school students regardless of the sexes/genders of the people involved. But I don't consider any of the work in Wishbone, *for instance, or in my new forthcoming book,* Small Fires, *to be "explicit." It's literature that has many themes, but one of the prominent themes is the exploration of gender and sexual identity. It isn't possible or desirable for me to parse myself, ever, in any context, into "the writer self" and "the gay self." They're entirely imbricated in both my life and work, and there's no way to get around that. So, for instance, if the principal says I can't come unless I don't "say anything gay," well, everything I say is gay because <u>I'm</u> gay. I don't have to be talking explicitly about my subject position, and I'm often not, but it's always there with me, and it's always part of anything I do or say or teach.*

Also, since Wishbone *just won the Lambda Literary Award for Lesbian Memoir, that's how the book is now explicitly coded. If Assumption isn't comfortable with the word "bastard" in a book title (even though the state of North Carolina stamped the word on Dorothy Allison's birth certificate!), then I'm not sure how comfortable they're going to be with an author speaking about a book that has just won an award with "lesbian" in the title. That may be something to consider. I truly believe—and I'm not saying that you would disagree with this, only that your employer might—that for all the conversations about heterosexual marriages and families that take place constantly around us, there needs to be an equal incorporation of the voices of all of us in equally valuable, equally meaningful families that happen to be organized around same-sex unions. And one way or another, I'm going to say that wherever I go, whatever the explicit subject matter I'm talking about.*

Sincerely yours,
Julie

9.

And then this happens: in February 2014, Angie and I are legally married in Washington State, in Bellingham where we first met and fell in love. The gathering is intimate, the restaurant candlelit, soft remnants of snow lining the streets and windowsills. Our paperwork is notarized by the county clerk without incident. Our names, unchanged, are united with an ampersand.

This is important to say: Though everyone we know insists that marriage changes a relationship, we find ourselves and our commitment unaltered. Perhaps this is because we have lived as unmarried married people for so long. Every night we have rested our heads on this pillow of paradox. *Married-but-not.* Every night we have covered ourselves with this blanket of paradox. *Unmarried-and-yet.* How do you take your coffee? *Black, with several packets of paradox, please.*

But we have access to the language of marriage now, and this is different. Where before we used *partner* to mean "like a spouse"—that elusive equivalency—now we use *spouse* to mean "a partner," unequivocally. In other words, our union has been upgraded from simile to metaphor.

"What's the difference between a simile and a metaphor?" I once asked my students.

The best answer: "Simile gets you on base, but metaphor knocks it out of the park."

~

We live in South Florida now, known for its oranges and oxymorons. Here in the Sunshine State, we find ourselves *Married-but-not,* a ban that states we cannot be what we are.

I carry a paper in my wallet that proves nothing about the nuances of love or the particularities of tenderness but marks instead a decision made by two consenting adults to go public as partners in this world. We signed the documents as a way of saying we are not single, and we are not straight. It was our way of showing we move "gaily forward" together, trying our best to be slow to anger and quick to joy.

After our wedding, I return to my job at a Florida state university. I log into the HR website and attempt to update my profile. *Yes, there has been a change to my marital status!* I unclick the box beside *Single* and click instead the box beside *Married.* For a moment, I feel the deep satisfaction of a private truth and a public truth aligning. I feel like a cartographer charting my own life at last.

But then when I go to enter the name and sex of my spouse, ERROR begins to flash on the screen, angry and insistent. I, a female employee, cannot designate a female spouse. INVALID ENTRY. The system is set up to make a liar out of me, to keep me "inned" and "pinned," to hold me in default mode.

When I write to the Director of Human Resources, she congratulates me on my wedding and then informs me that *unfortunately, you do not have a marriage as far as the state of Florida is concerned. We are closely monitoring the situation, however, and will let you know if anything changes.* She might as well have said: *You are suffering from an acute mental illness which makes you believe you are married.*

My heart is sharper than the diamond on my hand, but still the only word I can think of is *siege.*

~

I have never liked the word *wife*, and I never intended to use it in reference to myself, even if I one day had a husband. When I married Angie, I assumed we would call each other *partner*, just as we always had. But when you live in a land that tells you your marriage is a sham, an illusion, "merely symbolic," or worse, "a crime," you find yourself wanting to speak out, to refuse the relegation to *almost* or *nearly*, to answer nothing less than the whole question.

I call Angie my *spouse*, by which I mean we share a legally formalized life-partnership. We are *spouses*, which to my mind emphasizes the marital relationship irrespective of gender. Florida says I can have a same-sex partner but not a same-sex marriage. Florida lies. So I say *spouse* in part because I want to refute this lie, because I have always wanted to tell the whole story about my life without leaving anything out. In other words, without tucking anything back in.

I write to my parents before the wedding to say it is happening. They are silent. I write to my parents after the wedding to say it has happened. They are silent again. Silence is a cold war, but semantics, I have always known, cuts with swords and spikes.

A woman at the YMCA asks if I am married. I tell her yes. "Is your husband a member here?" she smiles.

A teller at the bank asks if mine is the only name on the account. I say there are two names, mine and my spouse's. "What's his name?" he smiles.

And so it comes to pass that I am inning myself inadvertently, with the same mother tongue I used to out myself before. "Just say *wife*. It's not ambiguous," a friend advises.

If I say *wife*, I compromise the truth that is in my heart. If I say *spouse*, I closet myself, in a world that still presumes marriage means heterosexual. If I say *partner*, I communicate the same-sex aspect of the relationship but not the fact that we are married. Florida wins again. It keeps us in our place—cloaked, shadowed.

Then, my father writes to say he and my mother are celebrating their forty-seventh wedding anniversary. He wishes I—*single* I—could be there with them at the beach. I notice the way he treads carefully around plurals, but not around the subject of marriage itself. My marriage isn't real to him, isn't real "in the eyes of the Lord." In other words, it is counterfeit, that which counts for nothing at all.

My father has a name: It's Florida.

His greatest sadness is that he feels like he "doesn't know me anymore." Perhaps this is code for *You don't take after me as much I thought, and given the way you've turned out, I am both relieved and disappointed.* One day, I'm going to have to divorce that surgeon in New England. It's hard to say which would cause a greater scandal: my being "gay," as in lesbian, or my being a "gay divorcée."

It's the wet season in Miami, so many sporting events are rained out. The green fields and the brown diamonds flood. The crowds run for cover. But every once in a while, there's a clear day, a blue sky, a perfect pitch: slow and smooth, the ball passing clean across the plate.

"So, how do you know Angie?" the clerk at the library asks.

I was always good at softball. Infer what you will. I choke up on the bat, blinking hard. I take a firm stance and a good swing. *CRACK.* I remind myself the game is just a metaphor.

"I'm married to her," I reply.

Meditation 36

I grow older

if I'm lucky.
And I'm lucky.

—Camille Rankine

If Miami is a unicorn, which of course Miami is—cloud-fringed and colorful, unbelievable to its core—then South Beach is the horn. Like most things, what we call a horn resembles something else. In this case, a pole. Picture the glittery whimsy of a carousel pole, the mirrored erotics of a stripper pole, the retro-aesthetics of a barber pole. Clutch them in your fist like pickup sticks. Now you're on South Beach. Walk with me.

I'm a woman in her mid-thirties—a poet, if that helps to place me on a spectrum of tunics and tangled hair, peasant blouses and scarves worn regardless of the weather. In fact, I have just come from a poetry workshop at the Hôtel Gaythering. This is not a typo. I'm a woman in her mid-thirties, but a lesbian in her early adolescence. I have been out of the closet for thirteen years.

It's a Saturday evening in July, which means a soft rain is spattering the umbrellas of the sidewalk cafés, a soft steam is rising from the pavement, and with it, a seductive hiss. The hard is here, too: disco, stilettos, buzzy neon signs. Many shih tzus and Chihuahuas wear fine jewelry around their necks. This part of Lincoln Road is closed to traffic. More people glide than schlep.

I have just stepped out of the macaron shop bearing six assorted cookies for my love. The box is lavender and prettier than anything I own.

"Excuse me, Mademoiselle!" A man leaps from beneath a storefront awning. I am a *Madam*, if you want to get technical about it, but there is no time. "A beautiful woman like you should be shielded from the rain." He opens an umbrella over my head.

This is all schmooze, I know. Perhaps even his accent is part of the charade. I smile, to be polite, though I am tired, en route to the parking garage, eager to cross the Broward County line.

"You are so beautiful," he says, unconvincingly. His dark eyes dart. He smooths his tie. "And yet, you could be much more so. Heads could turn as you pass by instead of following some other girl."

"But—" I want to say it doesn't matter. I'm a professor after all. Looking this way is one of the perks of my job.

"No buts! I have samples for you. They are must-haves. *Must-have!*" I am shaking my head, slowly retreating in my Toms loafers and Old Navy jeans. "But first, you tell me: what is your beauty regimen?"

No one has ever asked me this question before. *Regimen?* Like a system of government, strict and strategic.

"I don't have one," I murmur. Is it possible even his mustache looks aghast? I am striding away now, a vision in damp denim and adrenaline.

Monsieur calls after me: "But the blackheads! The fine lines!" More adamant in his last attempt: "The *sun damage!*" It is no use: soon, I am swallowed by the elegant maw of the crowd.

⁓

Sometimes I like to think I'm so enlightened about beauty products that I never buy them. Of course this isn't the whole story, and my spouse, in her knowing way, calls me to account. "You're just cheap," she says, "plain and simple." But I disagree. I consider myself discriminating, and tell her so, playfully. That is, I'd rather splurge on fancy coffees and hardbound books than purchase foundation to "conceal my pores," mascara to "plump up" my presumably wimpy lashes, or lipstick to "enhance my lip profile." Really? Is my mouth planning to post its resume on LinkedIn?

Still, beneath this snark and reticence, I'm responding, no doubt, to certain stubborn facts of my upbringing. Like many girls, I was raised by an appearance-conscious mother and a father who urged me to listen to her at all costs. "She knows about these things," he said when my mother gave me my first tube of lipstick as an eleventh birthday present. Like some girls, I was raised by a mother who equated being ugly with being undesirable to men, and told me so, often—a mother who in turn equated being undesirable to men with being a lesbian, that "most unspeakable thing." This was her special twist on the transitive property, which she revealed in a tearful uproar the first time she met the woman I love: "This is what you do!" my mother wept, pointing at my face, which was naked save for the new eyebrow stud. "This is how you make yourselves *ugly* for each other!"

Angie and I have laughed about her proclamation for years—*just how hideous do I have to be to turn you on, darling?*—but sometimes I hear my own laughter's hollow din, and I fear I make my jokes the way some mortals whistle in a graveyard.

Another strange fact: For all her concern with appearances, my mother never shaved her legs. They were hairless, smooth and shiny, two pale white candles that seemed to be made of wax. But she didn't wax them: not once, not ever. My mother never bought a bottle of Nair, never set foot in a beauty salon. My mother was take-care-of-your-own-business or bust. My mother was DIY before they invented the acronym. And even when my own legs began to bristle with sharp, blond hairs, she discouraged intervention: "If you shave, the hair will grow back thicker, darker. You'll be a slave to the razor all your life."

But, try being in eighth grade when you should be in seventh. Try believing there is a future of any kind after junior high, let alone an "all your life." The other girls have noticed the hair on your legs. They've started remarking about it, mostly stupid things like, "Hey, are you Little Red Riding Hood, or are you the Wolf?" But still. I'm a year younger, at least, than everyone else. I've been wading in puberty's shallow end, with only my acne and these stubby hairs to prove I belong at all. Then this: studying a paramecium under the microscope and realizing I have cilia, too. My legs resemble one-celled organisms, enlarged by the lens. They also resemble push brooms in the wrong light. Call the janitor and use me to sweep up!

Never mind that it doesn't make sense: You need to grow the hair to be able to shave it to be able to say it was there in the first place. "Pride and shame are kissing cousins," your future self will say. But you're not her yet. You haven't met any grown woman with hair on her legs or any grown woman who would allow it to remain. You haven't met any lesbians either, so you don't know they're just as divided on this issue as everyone else.

Resolved, you take a can of your father's Barbasol, one of his heavy-handled razors (not yet the disposable kind), and draw yourself a bath while your parents are outside tending the garden, grooming the unimpeachable front lawn. There's something going on at school that night—a pep rally or a talent show—and you can't have your paramecium legs, your push-broom legs, on display for everyone in the whole auditorium to see.

It looks simple enough in commercials: Coat your legs with cream, slide the razor seamlessly over the humps of your knees, swish it in water, then *rinse and repeat, rinse and repeat.* Only in commercials they never show the hair, never show the silver blades clogging so they can't cut anymore, never show how quickly and completely this occurs. The commercial legs are already shiny and smooth, as waxy and white as your mother's legs but without the dark veins, what you called as a child her "purple stars." They are the reason she doesn't wear shorts or skirts without pantyhose, why only you and your father have ever seen her in a swimsuit. Of childbirth, she laments: "It's not just a baby you're getting. It's *these* and *these*!"

You start at the ankle, and by mid-shin, you've dug in too deep, slicing the flesh, causing a high-pitched noise in your head. The bathwater becomes pink with your blood. When you look at the razor now, it's jammed again, but not with hair, with skin. *Your skin.* You've cut a piece as big as a dime, maybe a nickel or a quarter even. The pain is like fluorescent lights, flickering and whining at the same time. The blood pours out, thimble by thimble. You try to wrap your leg with a washcloth, but it doesn't do much. Then, you hear your mother stamping her feet on the doormat, calling for you from the entryway, wanting to know where you are. She is suspicious already, and she should be. You hunker down beneath the disappearing bubbles, hang your leg over the ledge, and wait. She'll patch you up, of course, but there will be consequences. There will also be a deep and enduring scar.

Sometimes the woman I love touches that divot in my shin. These more than twenty years, it has become a less-than-conspicuous thing. These more than thirteen years, her fingers still find it. I love when they pass over, and I love when they come to rest, as if sanctifying my lost self, the second navel that girl once cut.

Why did she do it? We can only speculate now: *Rebellion? Autonomy? Remembrance?*

Around the same time I started shaving my legs, I began writing an interminable novel called *The Curse of Beauty.* I doubt very much this is a coincidence. My favorite part of the writing enterprise was drafting the dramatis personae that would appear on the first page, even before the Table of Contents. "You know that's only for plays, right?" some Know-It-All at school said. I didn't even bother looking up.

My protagonist was a model named Angela Wilbourne: *She is seventeen and has already suffered for her beauty,* I wrote. Then, a salient parenthetical: *(5'9", 120 pounds, flowing blond hair and a willowy silhouette).* These words came from somewhere. They were not my own. Memory is a small boat: easy to rock, quick to tip over.

See my mother waving her copy of *Redbook* like a glossy flag: "Did you know that you and Nicole Kidman are exactly the same height? Just look at what a beauty she is: that *flowing blonde hair,* that *willowy silhouette!*" I was partial to Jodie Foster and Winona Ryder myself: women with sharp, astute faces and a whiff of melancholy about them.

This was the early '90s. The phrase "thigh gap" hadn't entered our cultural lexicon yet, but my mother was always ahead of the times. "See how her legs are as thin at the top as they are at the bottom?" Yes, I saw. Something to strive for, I guess. "And the spiral curls in this picture are so flattering, aren't they?" I nodded. For months, I would sleep in curlers secured with bobby pins, a prickling circumstance not of my own volition. But one day I would move far away, maybe to the East Coast, maybe even to Miami where you can be an old woman, funny and flawed, and they still let you tell stories on television. Of course neither of us knew this yet.

Deborah Wilbourne: *She is a dark, striking woman in a pinstripe suit. She manages her daughter's modeling career. Likely, she was married at one time, but her husband is absent from this story.* My mother wears a pinstripe suit to her job at the bank where she is building her second career. My father has a home office and a bathroom in the basement. He doesn't come to the table until he is called.

Jeffrey Blanchard: *Angela's boyfriend and a rising star on a primetime television program like* Melrose Place. *Jealous, possessive, and very good-looking. Rides a motorcycle. Resembles Grant Show from the actual* Melrose Place.

Wednesday nights when I am supposed to be brushing my teeth and applying Retin-A to my blemishes, I turn on the small television in the kitchen and watch as many clandestine minutes of *Melrose Place* as possible before my mother's voice rises through the vents, verifying my whereabouts and the progress of my preparations for bed. I guess I did have a beauty regimen once.

Valerie Hart: *Angela's best friend, who models for the same agency. She is a smart and free-spirited brunette with aspirations for college and a career in fashion. Valerie struggles to maintain her weight and is eventually dropped from the agency.* In parentheses, I have added an asterisk, a meta-aside: (*Valerie is the tragic character here. Despite her sense of humor and her insistence that beauty isn't everything, she will turn to drugs and eventually die by overdose or suicide. No one is sure which.*)

From 1994 to 1995, my parents and I watch the Fox series *Models Inc.* every week over popcorn and Diet Shasta. From 1995 to 1997, my best friend April and I stage a series of photoshoots around our neighborhood, wearing everything from formal dresses to two-piece bathing suits. I doubt very much this is a coincidence. After four hundred handwritten pages, I shove *The Curse of Beauty* into my drawer and never revisit it again. April suggests I should rescue the book, that I could make a happy ending if I chose.

"But that's where you're wrong!" I reply, full of righteous indignation, as if I am an expert on such things. "The real Cinderella was probably a Plain Jane. Disney just made her pretty to sell the story!"

~

In 1997, I leave for college. My small Christian university is only an hour from home, so my parents visit every weekend. During this time, my mother forms a friendship of convenience with the woman who oversees the cafeteria. Later, I will learn that Sally has been my mother's "eyes and ears," keeping a record of what I eat and with whom.

At one point during my freshman spring, I stop eating altogether. I say it has to do with Lent. I have become attracted to the idea of penance. I start sleeping on the floor beside my bed, "to remind myself what a luxury it is to have a mattress, a pillow, comfortable things." When my roommate travels, I climb into her bed, drunk on her scent and guilty after. I let the hair grow long on my legs, and sure enough, it seems darker and thicker than before. *What else*, I wonder, *will I be a slave to all my life?*

Today, at thirty-six, I marvel that I have reached my academic fulcrum: eighteen years before college, eighteen years since. My education continues apace. The truth is, college was my first serious relationship, the beginning of a lifelong romance. I fell in love with coffee carts and seminar class-rooms and designated quiet spaces. Sex in the university library was a long-recurring dream. I never saw my lover's face—man or woman, I couldn't say—but books rained down on us painlessly. They scattered everywhere, toppling from high shelves, spilling open to lines enjambed and end-stopped, stanzas and paragraphs interleaved. I can still hear them, rustling with the aftershocks of longing: *so much to learn, so much to know.*

These days, with my writing students, I often talk about the importance of dreams, accessing the imagery that most bewilders and beguiles us. "Dreams have their own internal logic, just as poems do, or lyric essays. It isn't that they 'don't make sense.' It's that they embody simultaneously that which we most want and fear to say."

Early memories may resemble dreams in this way. They are frequently vivid, visceral, and charged with feeling, but they materialize in isolation, lacking context or resolution. Recently, during an inclass freewrite, I fol-lowed my own advice and let my pen move ahead of my mind. I forgot, for a moment, the room I was in, the students all around me, and suddenly there I stood in a supermarket aisle: Albertsons, Seattle, Washington, circa 1985. I was myself, only smaller, and my little hand, which I recognized—the silver ID bracelet still loose on my wrist—reached out to touch the curls of colored hair pinned to the plastic trim in front of each box of dye. I loved them, those forelocks identical in shape and texture, varied only by hue. I had a habit of touching them, one by one. It was more than a habit really; it was a ritual. But here, now (*then, there*), I was stroking the dark auburn one, which must have been the color, in retrospect, that my mother used, semi-secretly, the reason we never saw her gray.

Anew, I remembered how my mother used to speak to me about coloring my hair. She made me promise that I would never "let myself go," which included a variety of failures—gaining weight, showing wrinkles, appearing in public without makeup—but notable among these was "letting myself go gray." My father had silver hair, which she considered "distinguished" for men and "disgraceful" for women. "If you show your gray," my mother warned, "you'll look like a witch, or worse—a *hippie*."

I remembered well how my mother's words struck like a gong in my chest, the deep fear they conjured, but I had long since forgotten the pure pleasure of stroking those curls in the supermarket aisle. This pleasure returned to me with a jolt thirty years later, and I was awed to discover that I had once savored deeply, if only for brief moments at a time, the idea of mutability; the freedom to change even the shade I wore in the world.

At the tail end of my twenty-second year, I came out to my mother. I had been living with Angie for three months already, not as roommates but as lovers. This was the truth I most wanted and feared to say. It was a truth I recognized with the vivid and visceral certainty of my own name. Still, I set the receiver down several times, choking on my own breath, before I finally dialed that most familiar number.

When you speak the unspeakable at last, a spell is broken. You are not who you were only moments before, but you are not who you think you are in that moment either. Call it the liminal space. Call it the katabasis. There is further descending, further unraveling to do. I was a woman who loved a woman, who had declared this love aloud. *Had I ever been heterosexual? Had I always been queer?* These were the wrong questions. I had lived all my waking life as a straight woman in a straight world, schooled in traditional expectations for courtship, marriage, and children with a man. I knew nothing yet of standing up to my waist in rip currents, of resisting a tide that insisted I must be otherwise—or that if I wasn't, I had better hide.

What is a lesbian life? What can it be? These are better questions, but the lesbian I would become was only, as yet, a distant glimmer in dreams.

A few years earlier, when my best friend turned twenty-one, she explained that she wanted to celebrate her birthday "fairy-tale style." At sixteen, April had begun taking ballet lessons and performing in small, local productions. She loved the leotards and tutus, the emphasis on grace and femininity. At eighteen, she competed to become a Seafair Princess, just as my mother had done three decades before. When she wasn't crowned a winner, April turned to collecting tiaras instead, sending away for them from catalogs until her bedroom transformed into a rhinestone temple. On a trip to Port Townsend, she had even purchased a vintage wedding dress that kissed the floor, at least a hundred white satin buttons trailing from nape to heel.

"Let's get really dressed up and go out in the world like a pair of beauty queens!" she said.

I shrugged. "It's your birthday. I'll do whatever you want."

Before dinner and the movie and the night with champagne and strawberries at a bed-and-breakfast (*how we fretted the proprietors would think we were lesbians!*), I drove us, at April's request, to the mall. She wanted to get her makeup done at the Clinique counter, that "most grown-up thing." My mother was only too happy to give me money, pleased by the good influence my longtime friend had turned out to be.

The woman who styled me was Kimberlee, with a double *e*. I remember telling her that I had never seen the name spelled that way before. "I like to be original," she said, dusting my face with powder.

Kimberlee, who resembled Stockard Channing from a recent Lifetime Original Movie, wore a tidy white smock and shiny black heels. They were at least three inches high.

"Don't your feet get tired?" I asked.

"It's worth it. Heels make your calves look like fine sculptures, long and lean. I think we ladies need all the help we can get."

Soon, she was plucking my eyebrows and lining my lips. There was some talk of "evening my skin tone" and "making my eyes pop." I saw how genuinely April was enjoying her consultation, and I wondered, genuinely, why it was so hard for me to enjoy mine. After Kimberlee showed me my "new face" in the mirror, she leaned in and whispered, "If you don't have a boyfriend yet, you will soon!"

~

Sometimes in televised sporting events, there's an instant replay and then a slow-motion replay, and then a big white line slices across the screen, circles the star athlete or the foul ball, indicating where everything went right or wrong. In memory, that's what happens when I think of this day: I see Kimberlee with the double *e*, her eyebrows plucked to stubs and drawn in with dark pencil—her lips too bright, her skin too white—a sad geometry of used sponges accumulating on the counter. And I see myself, twenty years old, comfortable at last in my jeans and sneaks and soft blue turtleneck sweater. Soon, I'll have to change, though, for the evening, and I'm dreading this already: the slip and the pantyhose and the shoes that call attention to themselves, clacking and clacking. I'm paying for something I don't want with money that isn't mine, and I don't even know why I'm doing it. I could have just waited for April, taken a stroll to the food court and back. There's always a Sbarro or a Panda Express when you need one, and I always keep a book in my bag.

Maybe I was just being "a good sport" that day. Or maybe I was trying something new, "opening myself to possibilities" like the checkout-line magazines urged me to do. But here comes that arrow gliding across the screen, pointing to the last words spoken in this scene, which are important. They reveal what the consultant presumed all of us were wearing this makeup for: "If you don't have a boyfriend yet, you will soon!"

I didn't have a boyfriend, but I wanted one, badly. In fact, I was appearance-conscious about this very absence. I felt the lack of a boyfriend made me look bad—worse, made me look *suspicious*. The truth was that I felt things for girls that I did not feel for boys, even for the boys I had dated. The truth was also that I could not admit those discrepancies in longing yet, even to myself. But then, the arrow; then, the line in the sand. I was not about to date any boy who wanted me to be a painted doll—who expected me, through the clothes I wore or the products I used, to make myself desirable to him—to curate his affections in some way.

This was not the day I came out of the closet. This was not even the day I recognized the closet I was in. But it was the day that gave way to the night when I scrubbed foundation from my face for the last time, smiled into the gold looking glass with the mermaid's tail, and mouthed the words I was just beginning to believe: *This is what a feminist looks like.*

Of course, I hasten to add, you can still be a feminist and wear makeup. We're not the Pore Police. You can still be a feminist and make your life with a man. We're not the Love Police either. All I can say is that I have needed feminism, as fraught and misunderstood a movement as it is, to grant me certain permissions I already possessed. To be my ruby slippers, if you will—or truer still, my red Keds.

~

Leap forward six years and find me knee-deep in the Pittsburgh snow, shoveling and shoveling. Our station wagon is sturdy, so we never skid on the ice. This feels like an accomplishment for two women who have not weathered real winter until now. In our trunk, we keep non-clumping kitty litter, bags of it—a copycat move after watching our neighbors pour the small gray pebbles onto their slushy driveway for traction. No one is going to find us stalled out on a side street between a thaw and a freeze, we resolve.

With this prolepsis, find me also knee-deep in partnership, knee-deep in my lesbian life. Angie and I are getting smart about things. We have wills that name each other, power-of-attorney forms notarized at the hospital. We have people we can call, in crisis or celebration, since our parents can no longer be trusted to pick up the phone.

This particular day we are pushing a cart through the crowded Giant Eagle. We turn down the soda aisle and find ourselves happily alone. A song I like comes on the store radio, and I start singing along, dancing the way I do in our kitchen at home. Angie rolls her eyes at me just as an employee rounds the corner. I pause mid-shimmy, looking down sheepishly. The man glances at me, then at my partner. He shakes his head as he chides: "Don't be like that. Your mother can dance if she wants to."

Then, we are howling with laughter. I take hold of a shelf to steady myself. All the air lodges in Angie's throat, and she can only gasp, desperate to release a breath. Hours later, recollecting this scene in tranquility, I muse aloud: "How does someone make a mistake like that?"

"He couldn't see your face," Angie sighs. "He was just judging from your clothes."

"So I dress like I'm old enough to be your mother?" I am twenty-six, a year younger than my love.

"Well . . . you've got a lot of colors going on there, a lot of layers—and frankly, a lot of holes." Angie states these facts like a witness in a jury box. She is not pleased to disclose them, but she is not particularly hostile either.

It was true that I had worn out the crotch of my sweatpants sometime before, but I had taken to wearing bike shorts underneath for cover. The shorts were black, the sweats were brown, the boots were beige and enormous—well-suited for any expedition I might decide to make across Antarctica. I wore a navy blue Carnegie Mellon sweatshirt that I loved and let the hood poke out over my cherished green coat, which came to my shins and was missing a button. I wore orange wool fingerless gloves and a multicolored hat with ear flaps, two braids of yarn that cinched under my chin. Some of these items were stained, I realized, and all of them were frayed, pilled, well past their wearing prime. I had not been to a clothing store for a very long time.

Suddenly, as I picture myself dancing in all that bright, mismatched raiment, I'm surprised the man didn't call for backup, that I'm not "under observation" in a psych ward right now. So comes the question I am both afraid to ask and afraid not to ask my beloved: "Are you ever . . . *embarrassed* to be seen with me?"

Angie, who has always loved me, indisputably, for exactly who I am, doesn't answer this question, not directly. "I think you're figuring out your style," she says. "You were never allowed to pick out clothes of your own until you got to college, and your mom made you wear makeup your entire adolescence, so this is your . . . *discovery* phase."

"But is it also maybe my . . . *homeless* phase?"

She looks at me, that knowing gleam in her eyes: "Well, put it this way: I wouldn't stand outside with a cup in your hand."

~

After coming out, I didn't wear a dress for ten years. I cut my hair short and clipped my nails down to the quick. I bought only men's jeans at thrift stores and one pair of khaki green Boy Scout pants—a treasured find!— that I wore until they finally disintegrated in the wash. All the photographs from this decade suggest that I reviewed everything my mother ever said about finding a man and keeping him, then did precisely the opposite. But the truth is, my transformation was never as deliberate as that. I wasn't trying to be "ugly"; I wasn't trying to make myself undesirable to men—any more than I was trying to make myself desirable to women. My feminist self didn't want her value as a woman to be contingent upon her looks, yet my lesbian self wanted to be recognized, and ultimately recognizable, for the kind of woman she was. This is the most vexing part about coming out: you know who you are at last! Perhaps you also know who you love! But no one else can see your queer truth, can know your queer heart just by looking at you. Even other queer people aren't sure. You can't always spot each other in a crowd, link arms, and form a circle that promises safety for everyone. Gaydar turns out to be just another unicorn, unbelievable to its core.

So you wish out of the sudden, overwhelming separateness you feel that you could slip a silver ID bracelet onto your wrist again. You have the old one in a jewelry box somewhere. It said your name and address in case you got lost, and then, inexplicably, *Lutheran*—another identity no stranger could see—this one selected for you by your parents at birth, finalized with a baptism at five weeks old. Then, you grew up, and the bracelet grew tight. You fell in love, but because you loved a woman and not a man, you found yourself lost in the world. What if you had a bracelet like that now, but instead of *Lutheran*, it said *Lesbian*? You could turn the bracelet over like the charm it was. People could see you coming, know who you were before you ever uttered a word. They would have to face you, you imagined, on your own terms.

~

My summer writing students are keeping a record of their dreams, which means that I am keeping a record of my dreams, too. Just before my thirty-sixth birthday, I have a doozy. I wake in the blue haze of not-yet morning and scramble to write everything down:

I dreamed my college roommate and my sister-in-law—both mothers of young children, pretty and patient in what seems an effortless way, and who have never actually met in waking life but who would like each other, I realize now—had conspired to throw me a party. I say conspired because I would never have consented to this kind of spectacle otherwise. They gathered everyone I knew, friends from work and the YMCA, for dinner and drinks at a nightclub. Not a coffee shop with cherry wood tables and frosted pastry cases. Not a diner with little jukeboxes and oversized booths. No, this was a full-blown Miami Beach discotheque, where toothpick women pranced on stilt-shoes, where men in half-buttoned shirts rippled and glistened in the heat.

"Surprise!" the guests shouted from the bar, raising their flutes and tumblers. I scanned the room for Angie but couldn't find her in the crowd. Becky and Kim stepped forward to present me with an old-fashioned envelope, complete with a candle-wax seal.

"We wanted to give you something *really special* this year." They spoke in slow unison, their smiles eerily wide.

I began to back away slowly, instinctively. I let the envelope flutter to the floor.

"It's a head-to-toe makeover!" they announced in sudden surround sound, and just then a spotlight appeared. Everyone dining at the nearby tables, grinding on the strobe-lit floor, turned their heads toward me to applaud.

Accompanied by chants of "It's about time!" and "You know that's right!" I bolted up the stairs, down a dark hall, through a long kitchen with skillets dangling over the chopping boards. I heaved my body against a steel door, burst forth into a cobbled alley. The dream had devolved into bad movie tropes in montage. Outside, two chefs in white mushroom hats smoked cigarettes against a grimy brick wall. Soon, it was raining, but every drop that fell was a mini black compact from CoverGirl.

At this point, I was frantic to get back inside, but the door had locked behind me when I came outside. "You'll have to go around!" one of the men called over his shoulder. But I didn't. Instead, I bent down and scooped up one of the tiny compacts in my palm. My mother had given me one of these, full-sized, when I started junior high, the C and G emblazoned in gold on top. I remembered it was supposed to help me "minimize the shine," but junior high took care of that on its own.

In the dream, my first impulse was to crush the compact under my foot, my second was to throw it with my strong outfielder's arm through one of the tall windows of the building next door. I wanted something to shatter, and I didn't want it to be me. But in the end, I slipped that compact inside my pocket. I felt it there, pressing against my palm, even as I woke. *Why,* I wondered, *did I take it with me, like a lucky penny found face-up on the ground?*

~

It turns out I do most of my best thinking in class—"on my feet," as they say, while wearing flats. The woman I have become, in her dark button-down with her tangled hair, is speaking now. I watch her move easily, comfortably, in front of this crowd.

"The best writing, regardless of genre, is rooted in mixed feelings. If your speaker or your character is certain about everything, where is the story? Why does it matter?"

We have been talking about a prose-poem that might also be a micro-essay by Marie Howe. It's called "What We Would Give Up," and college students seem to like it because it is about college students. I want them to be fond of themselves. More, I want them to recognize themselves in the words we read: *One morning in Orlando, Florida, I asked a group of college students—What would we be willing to give up to equalize the wealth in the world? [...] A car, the guy with the nose ring said. I don't have a car anyway.*

"It's always easier to give up something you don't have, isn't it? Easier than giving up something you have but don't necessarily want. Why do you suppose that is?"

"Because you think you might want it later; you might change your mind," one of my students says, eating ice cubes from a Starbucks cup.

"Yeah. It's like you feel bad that you're holding onto it, but you think you might feel worse if you let it go." Another student sips Red Bull through a bendy straw.

We consider the way the essay-poem ends: *Would I give up dyeing my hair? That was a hard one. If I stopped dyeing my hair everyone would know that my golden hair is actually gray, and my long American youth would be over—and then what?*

The speaker in Howe's essay-poem has so many questions, but then don't we all? She isn't able to answer any of them conclusively either: *Would I? Would I? Would I?* Hardest for her to imagine is letting her golden hair go gray—or more precisely, letting the gray that is hidden beneath it show through. She doesn't say she thinks she'll be ugly or unattractive to men or mistaken for a lesbian, that "most unspeakable thing." Maybe her hair was once golden all on its own, and she just wants to keep it as before. What does her "long American youth" mean to her, anyway? We can only speculate: *Rebellion? Autonomy? Remembrance?*

"You feel how torn she is," says a young man in a black T-shirt with a replaceable water bottle. "It's like she wants to be the kind of person who doesn't care about any of it, but she does care, and she's a little embarrassed that she cares, but at least she's honest about what she feels—and willing to write it down."

I nod. "Pride and shame are kissing cousins, aren't they?" The words seem to pronounce themselves first, then turn back for my blessing. "I think our finest work comes from the place where they kiss."

At thirty-six, I, too, am in love with my long American youth, which doesn't feel anywhere close to over. *Isn't it all a discovery phase?* I have dresses in my closet again, for those rare occasions when I feel like wearing them. My hair is long enough now to pin up or let down—long enough not to have to cut it so often. A few times, I've gone to T.J. Maxx with Angie and browsed the racks, found myself actually enjoying it—this shopping business—though I still keep a book in my bag.

All this is to say I have lived long enough now to understand that what I wear, or what I don't wear—my bare face, my shaved legs, the toenails I sometimes paint and sometimes don't—cannot possibly communicate to passersby anything certain about my lesbian life or even my feminist values. I think I may have a little witch in me after all, definitely a little hippie, too, but that doesn't mean I'm willing just yet to cede my *medium natural brown hair (Truffle)* to this rising tide of silver.

"I spent $6.99 on beauty products today," I tell my wife. Even my animosity toward this word is softening, the more I turn it over on my tongue. *Wife, wife,* rhymes with *life,* I tell myself. Maybe one day I will even be able to speak it aloud without cringing, make it as smooth as sea glass, hold it effortlessly on my tongue.

"Did you?" Angie smiles, pretending to be impressed. Or perhaps she really is.

"I bought Garnier Nutrisse Nourishing Color Crème, #50. I left a little gray at my temples—a tribute to my father, I guess—but I wasn't ready to be all the way gray so soon."

"I like it," she nods. "It's very . . . *natural.*" And then we both laugh at the absurdity of the word. Another true and false, another mixed feeling.

But wasn't there a moment just a few weeks ago when I stood in the Publix supermarket in Hollywood, Florida, in my Toms loafers and my Old Navy jeans, caressing the little forelocks lined up in a row? I didn't have to make a purchase. No one pressured me to report on my beauty regimen. I just saw a color I liked, a color that resembled my shade, and I took it home with me and made the little potion from the three containers combined into one. Then, I worked it through my hair into a thick, dark lather. I set the timer for twenty-five minutes and peeled off the plastic gloves. There was a simple, undeniable pleasure in every part of this process.

Then, I wandered into my writing room, a clip on my head, a towel slung casually across my shoulders. I wasn't exactly pleased with myself, but I wasn't exactly disappointed either. I typed a quote I like from a poem by Camille Rankine at the top of a blank page. Below it I put a bracket, some ellipses, a long dash—*and then what?*

Prose & Cons: Considerations from a Woman with Two Genres

I always thought, if I was lucky enough to be hired by a university—to be offered one of those elusive tenure-track jobs—my contract would say "Poet." The word would glow on the page, embossed and raised. It would gleam like the lone title on an old-fashioned movie marquee.

I am a poet first, I think. (I thought.) A priori.

I am lucky—some have the luck of the Irish, and I have the luck of the Poet. I thank my lucky stars.

A few years ago, I was hired by a university in sunny Miami. I was offered one of those elusive tenure-track jobs. The word "Poet" does not appear anywhere on my contract. I am an Assistant Professor of English with a specialization in Creative Nonfiction.

I was hired to teach my second language. I speak it fluently, I think. (I thought.) Still, a student stops me in the hall.

"You're a poet, right?"

"How did you know?"

"You can just tell," she says. "*I* can tell."

She has the shiny, black eyes of an owl, if owls wore a lot of mascara.

"But how?"

"I don't think a novelist would wear a shirt like that."

Prose & Cons: Considerations from a Woman with Two Genres

Apparently, I also have the shirt of a Poet.

~

I teach at a university with two Very Famous Poets. It is a strange thing to have come of age reading their poems, poems that bloom inside me like flowers inside globes. Have you seen those? They are so beautiful—irises and zinnias under glass.

The poem is the flower, of course. Prose the paperweight.

Now I sit across from these Very Famous Poets in meetings. They speak to me like I belong. They listen as I respond. Sometimes, I find I cannot stop blushing in their presence.

The poem is the pink heat, of course. Prose is the cheek.

~

It takes two weeks before my Intro students admit they have no idea what I mean by *PROSE*.

"Do you mean like—pros and cons?" the shy boy in the back row asks.

"No." I smile. "Not PROS—PROS*E*," adding the "E" with a blue dry-erase marker. "See—it has a *rose* in it." (*Is Poetry the rose?*)

"So when you say we have to submit a work of prose—"

"I mean, a short story or a personal essay." I cringe as I feel the phrase coming, cresting the hill of my tongue. "For the first workshop, you will submit a poem and something that is not a poem—a work of prose."

And here we are, stalled out in Binary Station.

~

My first publication was a poem. It marked the beginning, I thought, of my public life as a poet. A Very Famous Poet whose work I admire chose my poem as the winner of a prize.

I was so lucky. I was poet-lucky. I thanked my lucky stars.

Technically, though, my first published poem was a "prose-poem." Notice how we never say this the other way around—a "poem-prose." The phrase falls awkwardly on the ear, so we dismiss it. This is our poetic prerogative—to lead by sound. Perhaps this is what makes a prose-poem more poem than prose. (Perhaps.)

My small block of text—with its close attention to sound, its close inspection of language itself—would never have been published as prose. It would not have qualified as a "short story" or a "personal essay." There were no characters; there was no plot; my text was lacking a reflective narrative centered in self-discovery and growth.

In other words, it was more poem than prose. See, I'll show you:

Y

Little letter I could not love. Vowel & consonant, chromosome & question. How frugal & elusive you have been! Always the middleman: *xyz, xyz*, never the workers or the bourgeoisie. Also the musicman: *xylophone & lyre*. At times I find your histrionics almost unbearable—a new age of *womyn & wyne*. Too haughty for the twenty-fifth place, you stand like V on a stilt, on a pedestal stair, touting your yowling message. Inverted tripod. Impotent slingshot. (David's one-time triumphant tool.) & what a spy you are, your cunning infiltrations: *dys-trophy, dys-functional, dys-phoria*. How could I ever catch you? Stealthy somnambulist, chameleon of stick limbs & curlicues. You reduce nouns to improper adjectives with these easy recipes: *smirk-y, pith-y, weight-y, greed-y. Lad* into *lady*. That's your fix, your sing-song-y resonance. Usurper of the second person. Pseudonym for stranger. You & yours assaulting me & mine through triangle lips split open. Isosceles. Take your tuning-fork face & turn it into the light. Make your inquiry, outspoken & asinine. *Yawn, yang, yammer*. An active force in the universe. Tell me I'm boring you. Call me *yellow*. Tempt me with *yams*, sweetened to marshmallow pudding. Or come in second: *axis, coordinate, unknown quantity*. Occasionally, impressed with your arrogance, I've let you *yo-yo* me—lift up my skirts, my songs, *buoy* me again in the wrong direction. Invention: the crafty voice in the back of the head, making suggestions. Or the picture on the grade school wall, building associations. *Y is for yak*, a long-haired, humped Tibetan ox & *you* who are never what you are.

~

If a prose-poem can win a POETRY contest but the same prose-poem cannot win a PROSE contest, what is this but another form of identity politics?

~

I am a poet. I am also a lesbian. These are two irrefutable truths about me. Some would save space and call me a *lesbian poet*. (No one has ever called me a *poet lesbian*.) *What is the relationship between these words?* I wonder. They are neither synonyms nor antonyms. One is neither the cause, nor the effect, of the other.

~

An old joke: *If you're a poet, where's your license?* Is it true that

Think of the SATs I have taken, think of the GREs—I have been trained to think in analogies.

lesbian : poetry :: heterosexual : prose

~

I like the double colon better than the equals sign. It suggests that relationships can mirror each other without being equivalent.
:: I was always a better student in language arts than math.
~ Notwithstanding, I did have a fondness for story problems.
~ All story problems are not classes, but all classes are story problems.

~

Back at Binary Station, the students linger on the platform, equal parts earnestness and ennui.

"So, you're saying a poem is that which is not prose, and prose is that which is not a poem?" (God bless and curse at once my student philosopher.)

No, I'm not saying that. The language forced me into it. The language is fond of boxes.

"You're saying they're mutually exclusive?" he asks again, the philosopher in the ratty plaid hoodie.

A train is speeding through the station now. The train's name is printed in bold, black letters: **TAUTOLOGY**.

In other words: no matter what I say, I will be right in some sense and wrong in another.

I think I write poems because I cannot tell the whole story. I think I write prose because I want to.

All aboard! the conductor calls.

~

A train track is 300 miles long. On one end of the track, Train A leaves the station at 4 p.m. On the opposite end of the track, Train B leaves at 6 p.m. If Train A travels 45 miles per hour and Train B travels 60 miles per hour, when will they meet?

~

My lack of interest in the correct answer to this question assures me I am not a mathematician. But—I have other questions.

The poet in me wishes to feel the train in motion, to sample a meal in the dining car, to glimpse the scenery from a small compartment window. I may also wish to compare this motion, this meal, this scenery with other kinds.

The prose writer in me wishes to know the passengers' names and what weather they are dressed for and if there are lovers on board who will be reconciled at some undetermined hour.

~

Nota bene: Story problems involving time, distance, and speed can be hard to solve because they involve multiple variables.

~

Earlier, I proposed the following analogy:

lesbian : poetry :: heterosexual : prose

What I wish to consider: *If this is true, how is it true?* (Now *I* sound like a philosophy major.)

    1. *Lesbian* and *poetry* represent categories that deviate from standard expectations, while *heterosexual* and *prose* represent categorical norms.

        1A. More people than not are heterosexuals.
        1B. More writing than not is prose.

A Poet-Question: *Why is poetry so comparatively rare? (And lesbians, for that matter?)*

    2. *Lesbian* and *poetry* specify categories that are not valued in the same way or to the same degree as the categories *heterosexual* and *prose*.

        2A. The former are less lucrative, in all respects.
        2B. The latter are less controversial, in all respects.

A Lesbian-Question: *Why is a heterosexual life never referred to as a "heterosexual lifestyle"?*

    3. To announce oneself as a lesbian or a text as a poem will result in raised eyebrows.

        3A. Eyebrows may be raised for many reasons, including curiosity, contempt, both, or neither. But eyebrows inevitably arch in the presence of these words. There is something (almost) (always) dangerous about them.
        3B. Heterosexuality and prose do not require an announcement of any kind. They are assumed. Even when they are not understood, they are assumed to be understood because they are expected to be ordinary.

A Poet-Lesbian-Question: *Why am I (almost) (always) drawn to marginal forms?*

~

The passengers grow restless on Tautology Express. I hear my own voice struggling to overcome the static on the PA system:

> "I don't want to say there are no differences between poetry and prose, but I don't want you to mistake them for simple opposites either. They have much in common. Often, they overlap. They are more like friends than rivals—in the best cases, they are allies. But even you and your best friend have perspectives that diverge, priorities that divide you, desires that perforate your otherwise symmetrical seams. If you and your friend witnessed the same event, would you give identical accounts of what happened? Poetry and prose are two ways of witnessing the same event—the event of a life, let's say, the event of being in the world. These accounts may dovetail with each other, but they will never read, nor should they read, the same."

~

In the multi-genre class, we are preparing for our first workshop. A challenge I have noted in providing feedback to others is how to be precise about what we mean.

"One of the most popular descriptors I've encountered in your peer responses is the word *poetic*," I say. "A lot of people are telling each other, 'This is very poetic.' I see the phrase written beside particular lines of poetry and alongside whole passages of prose. But what do we mean when we call something *poetic*? Is it a compliment? And if so, what kind of compliment?"

The girl with the bright owl-eyes perches in the front row. "It's a positive thing for sure," she says. "It means the writing is beautiful."

"But what does beautiful mean? Aren't there many ways to be beautiful?"

"*Lyrical*," another girl clarifies. Before I can intercept this word, she passes it to a classmate, a friend who says, "*Musical, melodious, rhythmical*."

We volley.

"So, you're telling me that *poetic* means the writer is paying particular attention to sound, to the intricacies of the language?"

They nod as one head—their beautiful, rhythmical faces.

A sudden surge of pride—this poet's license, burning a hole in my pocket.

Now a hand shoots up in my periphery like a blade of grass. He has a crew cut and a Trapper Keeper, like he is from another time.

"If *poetic* is the word for when something is like a poem—musical and all that—what's the word for when something is like prose?"

poetry : poetic :: prose : _____

"Does anyone know?" I ask.

They shake their serious heads.

"*Prosaic,*" I say. "But I'm not sure this word is terribly useful to us. It sets up an unpleasant antagonism between what is poetic and what is not—a false hierarchy. Instead, we could ask: *What* are the qualities of prose that make it valuable? What are the pros of prose?"

I laugh a little at my own wordplay, but my redirection is no match for the iPhones in the room. I have trained my students to look up words they don't recognize, and all at once, a new chorus of voices resounds.

"The dictionary says prosaic means dull, unimaginative."

"Mine says commonplace and unromantic."

"Pedestrian."

"Matter-of-fact."

"Lacking poetic beauty."

I think of my contract a moment, of a phantom clause: *You have been hired to teach unbeautiful writing. You are a specialist in unbeautiful words.*

"Did anyone find a more neutral definition?" I ask.

The philosophy major: "*Having the style and diction of prose,*" he says, but there is a sullen note in his tone.

~

By way of analogy:

"So, you're gay!" a new acquaintance exclaims after I explain I have a partner, not a husband.

I nod and press a second button on the antiquated elevator. Never fond of boxes, I take some small comfort in the fact that this one moves.

"That must be so exciting!" she sighs. "I can't imagine . . . me, with my boring little life."

I force a smile and look away. Her eyes continue to sweep over me—eagerly, curiously. She means no harm, yet there is something of the voyeur about her. I am certain I saw her eyebrows rise.

"It's just an ordinary life," I say as the doors slide back to let me pass. "No more or less ordinary than yours."

lesbian : poetry :: heterosexual : prose

~

Let's try this:

There are two trains, P_1 and P_2, running on parallel tracks toward a common destination. We might call this, for the sake of a name, Literary Junction. One question to consider is the importance of the destination at large— what must all trains accomplish if they are to succeed in their course?

The transportation of passengers from one place to another.

I suggest all readers are passengers. I submit transporting us from one place to another is what all good literature does.

A further question to consider is how we recognize the trains when we see them from a distance. Before I have even heard the whistle, what reasonable estimates can I make about the platform on which I should stand?

Prose & Cons: Considerations from a Woman with Two Genres

"Are you asking how we recognize a poem, the visual cues that distinguish it from a work of prose?" (Gratitude for the young anthropologist with her keen, studied speech, the pencil perennially stashed in her hair.)

"Yes. That is what I'm asking, exactly."

~

Nota bene: Story problems involving appearance, identity, and representation can be hard to solve because they involve multiple variables.

~

"I thought poems were written in stanzas and prose was written in paragraphs." (Binary.)

"But what about those big bulky poems that look like a paragraph someone forgot to indent?" (Devil's advocate.)

"That's a prose-poem. It isn't exactly the same; it looks like prose but moves like poetry. It's a mixed text." (Bitextual?)

"I don't know what you're all so worried about. If I don't know what it is, I just look up the genre. It's usually printed somewhere—in a header or an index or on the back cover of the book. Nobody publishes anything as unmarked territory." (Notice how we only travel to places with names.)

"So, are you telling me that there is nothing intrinsic about a poem's poem-ness, or the prosiness of a work of prose? The designation is the thing that makes it so?" I ask.

The philosophy major, calling my bluff, blowing the whistle on this whole charade: "Well, there's nothing intrinsically *Evan* about me, but that's the name I answer to."

~

An old rhyme: *You're a poet, and you didn't even know it.*

Can the same be said of a poem, a work of prose? Could anyone or anything be something without knowing that was what they were?

Or worse—was it possible we really were nothing without names?

This was getting downright biblical, I thought. (I think.) Were we all amorphous creatures until some Adam at a lit mag or a publishing house notarized and particularized us into a certain kind of existence, a social genre?

To name, of course, is also to stratify.

~

I ask my students, "Can there be a poem that doesn't look like a poem? What about a story that doesn't resemble any story you've ever seen before?"

"Is the text disguised for some reason, intentionally misleading?"

"No, let's say it just doesn't announce itself in conventional fashion."

A pensive student with a head scarf answers. "I think, at the end of the day, the text has to reveal itself and how it wants to be read. The reader can guess, but she can't know for sure without confirmation from the text—which really means the author." (Contract with the reader.)

~

God the Author said, "Let there be a vault between the waters to separate water from water" (alt. *poem from prose*). So God made the vault and separated the water under the vault from the water above it. And it was so. God called the vault *sky* (alt. *poem*). And God the Author said, "Let the water under the sky be gathered to one place, and let dry ground appear." And it was so. God called the dry ground "land" (alt. *prose-poems*), and the gathered waters he called "seas" (alt. *prose*). And God the Author saw that it was good.

~

Nota bene: *Creation is the ultimate story problem.*

~

Earlier, I proposed the following analogy:

lesbian : poetry :: heterosexual : prose

Prose & Cons: Considerations from a Woman with Two Genres

What I wish to consider: *the question of visibility.*

For instance, if there is a poem that doesn't look like a poem, who is to blame? Should the poem be absorbed into the canon of prose because it has failed to distinguish itself as something else?

Or perhaps the standards for how we recognize a poem should change. Are the boundaries arbitrary in some sense? Are the limits oppressively narrow?

~

My poems don't always look like poems. I don't always look like a lesbian. Two irrefutable truths. I have some sense of the form each entity (identity) is supposed to take.

I suspect there is some desire for subversion in the way I make a poem and in the way I make myself. This may be more conscious at some times than others.

The broadest meaning of a poem, poïesis, is "to make." There is no designation in the ancient Greek for how this making must occur or for the shape the final poem must assume.

When I called my mother to tell her I love a woman, she screeched like a bird: "This explains why you don't wear makeup!"

Apparently, I have the shirt of a Poet and the bare face of a Lesbian. *I have marked myself unwittingly*, I think. (I thought.) I have even marked myself, in some sense, by what I am missing.

When I called my friend to tell her I love a woman, she wept like Mary kneeling before the cross: "Your love can never make a baby!"

I ask again: *Are the boundaries arbitrary in some sense? Are the limits oppressively narrow?*

~

As you go about your daily routine over the next few days, begin to pay attention to places where you notice poetry or what you recognize as poetic language. Sometimes I find poetry in unexpected places: a Facebook post by someone I hardly know, a brochure I pick up while waiting in line, notes on bulletin boards, bathroom stall graffiti. Please bring with you to class <u>at least 2 examples</u> of what we might call "found poems." (If you can't bring the poetic text with you in its original form, type it up and bring a hard copy that you can share.) Remember that what makes these poems "found poems" is that they are not labeled explicitly as such. You as their reader discovered them in a non-poetic context; you *found* them and recognized something about them that led you to believe they were poems.

~

By way of analogy, this memory:

"Oh, I've always thought you were gay," Sophia says. She is the ex-girlfriend of my ex-boyfriend, who we both are certain is gay.

"What makes you think so?" We smoke clove cigarettes at a coffee shop in Eugene, Oregon—both of us poets invested in appearing so.

"It's a vibe," she shrugs. "It's the way you move, and the way you sound, but not one thing only—a lot of things together that form a gestalt." (Sophia, for the record, is also a psychology major.)

"A gestalt of gayness?"

She shrugs again. "Why not?"

"Well, I mean, I've only dated guys, so I'm pretty sure I'm straight. Do you think my vibe could be bisexual?" (Prose-poem?)

Sophia tosses back a dark espresso, cringes as the sludge slides down her throat. *Poets drink espresso, right?* Finally, after a long pause (caesura)— "Yeah, I don't see it."

"But what is there to see?" My mouth is frothy with cappuccino foam. *Poets drink cappuccino, right?*

Then, revising (backpedaling?): "Anyway, the heart is like a pendulum. It always swings both ways."

We're poets after all, self-professed. We like to speak in similes.

"But the body's a revolving door," she says. "It always comes back around to one lobby."

Metaphor: the ultimate one-upmanship.

~

My students find poetry everywhere—grocery lists, menus, instruction manuals. Poetry hovers in the air—overheard conversations, natural sounds mingling with human voices. Snippets of the world whirring past, glimpsed as if from a small compartment window:

> *Rainier cherries. Brussels sprouts. Red wine for tea.*
> *Two hummingbirds at a feeder and today's pages done.*

> *Best part of the day. Driving home and a turtle in the road.*
> *I stopped and helped her on over to the other side and she hissed,*
> *even from inside her shell. Good for her.*

> *Man at the farmers' market eating huge bites out of a whole*
> *yellow tomato: "Now that tastes real, for a change."*

"We should do this with prose!" a zealous boy exclaims, scratching his lightly stubbled chin.

"You can't, silly!" his girlfriend chides. "Prose doesn't get lost, so why would we need to find it?"

~

I am a poet first, I think. (I thought.) A priori.

But I was wrong. No one is a poet first. You can be a poet *next* and *last* and *best*. It can become the truest thing about you—irrefutable.

Prose is always the first language.

~

We have gathered in the dining car of our final class party to sample a meal of chips, soda, and someone's roommate's hand-dipped, chocolate-covered oranges. "They're really good, I promise," she tells the class.

"So the found poem surprises us because it pops up someplace it isn't supposed to be—or at least someplace it isn't expected to be?" I begin.

"Like a weed."

"Or a flower."

Cue dueling similes.

"Do we need poetry?" I ask my students after a while. "What purpose does it serve if most everything we say and read and write is prose?"

They are quiet—contemplative perhaps, or merely tired.

Finally, a freckled English major raises his hand, wipes his mouth, and volunteers. "Our textbook talks a lot about patterns, but [Heather] Sellers says you have to break them sometimes, or the writing becomes predictable. Poems break the rules of prose, you know. They change the game or shift the focus. They're disruptive, but in a good way."

Now the anthropologist: "The prose-poem kind of seems like an oxymoron to me, you know? Because there's a lot of poetry in prose anyway, and vice versa. All the poems we found were just embedded in some larger context we'd call prose. And who was that guy who said the thing about *'Always be a poet, even in prose'*?"

"Baudelaire." I smile.

"Yeah, him. That's what the prose-poets are doing already, consciously, and what the found poets are doing unconsciously."

Now the philosopher: "I'm not disagreeing with you exactly, but we can't be naive about this either." He suddenly seems very old for nineteen, but his fingers, twisting the strings of his ratty plaid hoodie, are notably young.

"What seems naive to you, Evan?"

"Well, you know how you're always passing around that magazine, *Poets & Writers*? It might be redundant in some ways, but the whole publishing industry obviously thinks there's a distinction. I mean, if there weren't, wouldn't the magazine just be called *Writers*?"

Prose & Cons: Considerations from a Woman with Two Genres

"But poets *are* writers," the journalism student insists.

"Sure, but when we hear the word *writer*, we think *prose*. It's automatic. We probably don't even realize we're doing it, but if someone says to me, 'I'm a writer,' I think he means he writes novels or stories or maybe a memoir or something. He might even be a journalist. But for some reason, I'm not going to expect him to be a poet unless he says, 'Hey man, I'm a poet.'" (Or wears the shirt of a Poet?)

~

Before I built a wall I'd ask to know
What I was walling in or walling out,
And to whom I was like to give offence.
Something there is that doesn't love a wall,
That wants it down.

~

And yet, just as often:
Good fences make good neighbors.

~

"You think everything is about identity politics," my partner laughs.
But what if everything is?

~

By way of analogy, a reverie:

If my best friend had written to me while I was studying overseas, she would have filled the aerogram cautiously with her small, precise script. She would have written instead of using her international calling card, preferring my response to come slowly, if at all.

Dear J—,

I can picture you traveling by train all across the United Kingdom. I'm a little jealous, actually, of your freedom, even though I know it is only yours for a short time. I'm curious too about the girl you've mentioned in your correspondence. The way you describe her makes her sound like more than a friend. (I'm sure I'm just imagining things here, but you never write anymore about what's happening with you and Ben . . .)

I've made some decisions since graduating in winter term. N. and I will move to California this summer where I plan to teach and establish residency. Then, I'll go for my Master's degree in creative writing. All the applications ask you to specify your genre, and while I know you think of me as a poet because of all the poems we've exchanged over the years, I have decided to become a fiction writer and apply in prose. Unfortunately, poetry isn't practical as part of a career. It's a lovely idea, of course, but most poems end up in shoeboxes under a bed somewhere, and I want to have a real life as a writer.

I hope this doesn't disappoint you too much. I would never want to do anything to dampen your dreams, but it is important to think realistically about the future.

Love,
K—

P. S. We have set a date for the wedding, and we would like it very much if you could read a poem for us.

~

I collect my students' final genre consideration papers. Climbing into my car, I think nostalgically of trains—of reading while someone else navigates the tracks.

When I get home, I begin to leaf through the papers, noting moments of insight and thoughtful inquiries.

I think I am a poet because of my long love affair with questions. I think I am a writer of prose because of my deep infatuation with answers.

~

Previously, I thought poetry was a work in which words rhymed, the lines were compressed, and it was limited to a way of telling someone how you felt. But now I understand that poetry is so much more than that; it's not only a way to express your emotions, but a way to tell a story, a way to transform something devastating or ugly and turn it into something beautiful. Poetry is more about the words than it is the rhythm, in my opinion. A rhythmic flow lets the reader know they are reading poetry, but the words let the reader know the story or the reason you are writing the poem.

—Dwight Tracey, Jr., student in Introduction to Creative Writing

⁓

What makes poetry different from other genres is its rhythm. Whether it is apparent or subtle, poetry has a music that drives the words. Similar to lyrics in a song, poetry can be read melodically. The prose poem is something I was not too familiar with before taking this class, but I am now interested in writing a few of my own. Like I mentioned before, I find that prose poetry differs from regular prose because of its rhythmic sound. On the surface, it can be quite difficult to differentiate the two, but upon further investigation, it is clear that the prose poem, like a poem, carries that subtle rhythmic sound.

—Stephanie Diaz, student in Introduction to Creative Writing

⁓

What was also so interesting to learn is that poems and prose could sometimes intertwine and hide within each other, making it almost impossible to tell which is which.

—Crystal Falloon, student in Introduction to Creative Writing

⁓

One student leaves me a notecard tucked in his pocket folder. "I found this definition in an online dictionary," he writes. "I know you want us to do our own thinking about this, but I still liked what the dictionary had to say."

Poem: *A piece of writing that partakes of the nature of both speech and song, and that is usually rhythmical or metaphorical.*

⁓

Earlier, I proposed the following analogy:

lesbian : poetry :: heterosexual : prose

What I wish to consider: *the question of hybridity.*

4. The categories lesbian and poetry partake of the categories heterosexual and prose in that they require the existence of these categories in order to differentiate from them.

4A. A lesbian begins life as a de facto heterosexual, then blossoms divergently.
4B. A poem begins life as de facto prose, then blossoms divergently.

Both of these, flowers inside globes.

5. The lesbian and the poem are, by nature or necessity or some combination of the two, experimental beings.

5A. Given the heterosexual imperative, there are very few Gold Stars.
5B. Given the prose imperative, there are very few poets who have not also written a paragraph.

By contrast, a great many heterosexuals and prose writers have not explored another genre.

6. The lesbian and the poem are manifestations of multiple languages, or perhaps multiple versions of the same language.

6A. The lesbian descends from heterosexuals; they are part of her ancestry, as she is part of their lineage.
6B. The poem draws words, sounds, and images from the same unfathomable well as prose.

Not opposites then, not even analogies. What would we call this—symbiosis?

～

Nota bene: At the end of the day, I am a lesbian. I am a poet. I am a lesbian poet, or a poet lesbian. During the day, some days, I write prose. Some days, I go to the movies and weep when the boy loses the girl and when the boy finds her again. I understand that love crosses genres. I move in a world populated by prose and heterosexuals. I understand these forms predominate, but they are not less or more than my own. I am born of heterosexuals, after all. They are in me, I am of them—the way prose is in me, too—and I am fashioned out of prose. At the end of the day, I am a found poem.

~

A Very Famous Poet comes to my door. She brings me volumes of her words: a gift, an offering: poems and prose-poems. Further evidence of my outstanding inheritance.

In one book, she has written:

For Julie—the woman with two genres!

With deep admiration for your poems and nonfiction!!

I am so lucky. I am poet-lucky. I thank my Lucky Star.

Meditation 38

1.

In early life, Operation is the everywhere game on tables and rumpus room floors. The patient is supine and naked, red-nosed and round-bellied. Alone, he embodies the world.

What we know so far: *Man equals body.* His condition: space-taking, un-equivocally physical. Children do not have bodies yet. We wait for ours like coming attractions—in doorways, at desks, on the lawn.

Though our mothers and teachers carry their lives in bodies, like women before them carried water from wells, we learn their bodies are not equal to men's. This is why men lead women around by the elbows, steer them with a light hand on the lower back, the way a rudder steers a ship.

We are young, but we have eyes in our not-yet bodies. We are small, but we see everything.

I blush when I gaze at the board-game man. I blush at his big head, his big ears, the bulk of him. I blush at what should be there but isn't—one bulge that divides us all into separate lines and locker rooms. So much fuss over something that can simply disappear.

He should get dressed, I think. *He should put on his clothes and go home.* No one wants to be cut, no one wants to be probed, not even in make-believe.

The fact is, if I think too long about bodies, if I imagine what goes on inside them—for instance, if I dwell on the scummy rim that appears where the bathtub was white only moments before—I won't be able to stop. I'll feel my heartbeat everywhere but inside my chest, everywhere but where it belongs.

"Your turn," they tell me. I pick up the tweezers, the prongs, whatever they're called. *Is this the way real doctors reach inside a body?* Clutching them, I touch the sides of the cavity, which are out of bounds. A beeping that is hot in my ears, that burns through me: I drop the tweezers, the prongs, whatever they're called. The other kids squeal. *Never steady, never ready.* Again, I fail to lift the butterflies out of his stomach.

2.

My mother recounts how, upon seeing my father the very first time—at Sears, Roebuck and Company in 1963—butterflies stirred inside her stomach. He passed by on an escalator, his back turned, his eyes turned. He was tall and lean with limbs that suggested a great wingspan.

"It's just like they say," she says. "So many butterflies I could hardly breathe."

My father never says if, or when, he looked back. My father never says if, or when, the butterflies inside his stomach stirred.

3.

When I begin to swim at the Southwest Community Center, there is one season when no one else enrolls in lessons. Coach Gary meets me by the side of the pool but never climbs into the water. He has taught me before. He is confident I will not drown. Still, as we both recall, I am not his favorite student.

"Different bodies lend themselves to different strokes," he says. His swim trunks are loose and red. His chest is flat and downy with hair. His biceps bulge. "You have long limbs, which makes you better suited for some strokes than for others."

We have been over this before. I like the breaststroke best, which is for shorter bodies, squatter bodies, those darting little tadpoles in the pond.

Coach Gary motions for me to stretch my arms wide as I slip into the shallow end. "With a wingspan like that, you're a natural for backstroke," he says. "And someday, with practice, you'll be ready for butterfly."

To prove his point, he binds my ankles with a rubber strap and hands me a board. I swim lap after lap of the butterfly kick, learning—like the good girl I am—how to keep my legs together.

4.

Always, *natural* is a word that troubles me. The way it cuts and probes. The way it beeps inside my head with a hot burning.

Who is this *natural woman* Carole King sings about? And why isn't she Carole *Queen*?

I listen to her lyrics and parse them in my mind:

The woman doesn't feel *natural* on her own. Someone else—this man— this man who named the song and wrote it with her, with King—he's *the key to [her] peace of mind.*

But it wasn't just her mind that didn't feel *natural.* It was her body, too— something hollow there, some kind of lack. Perhaps there were no butter- flies fluttering in her gut. He makes her *feel so good inside.* He brings the butterflies.

I am most troubled by the lines:

> *I didn't know just what was wrong with me,*
> *'Til your kiss helped me name it.*

So, a woman alone is unnatural, and any woman without a man is alone?

Aunt Linda likes the song, the slow version on a black record in a grainy sleeve. Aunt Linda is a woman without a man.

In the den, pushing the needle back again, she says: "Julie, don't you ruin this song for me with overthinking. No one in our family overthinks things, and we all got along just fine before you started sticking your big brain in."

5.

All my life, people have been keen to comment on how big I am. *Big-boned, big for my age, too big for the kiddie rides, too big to order from the kids' menu.* My mother corrects them, indignant: "You mean *tall*," she says. "My daughter isn't *big*; she's *tall*." I begin to doubt the difference.

With my big brain, I collect big words. I pluck them like fruit from over- burdened trees. The language is an orchard I roam with basket in hand.

Collected: *Anomaly,* meaning exception, peculiarity; a deviation from the common rule, order, or form. In my head, I hear *animal-ee*, possessing qualities of an animal; carnal.

Collected: *Sui generis*, Latin for *of its own kind*, in a class by itself, unique. In my head, I hear *soo-E*, what the farmer calls to summon the hogs.

Collected: *Xenogenesis,* meaning the generation of offspring entirely different from their parent or source. In my head, I hear a silence that is not a grave, a silence in which I begin to live.

6.

At school, we are learning about butterflies. First, there are pipe-cleaner caterpillars. Later, wings formed from brightly colored tissue paper. The process is simple but satisfying. I like how, even after the wings are added, you can still see what the butterfly was before. The caterpillar remains a linchpin, a knot for the unfolding bow.

The presence of the caterpillar within the butterfly is not unlike certain baby pictures where a classmate still resembles herself, only shorter, squatter. On the bulletin board, for instance, everyone can always spot Janna: same moon face and bulging eyes.

My picture takes even the teachers by surprise. *Where did all that black hair come from? And that snow-white skin! Are you sure that's even really you?*

We learn most butterflies lay their eggs on leaves. We learn most butterflies lay many eggs at once; they are small but finely sculpted. Together, they resemble a honeycomb, dense and gleaming with potential. Perhaps this is hyperbole for hyperbole's sake. Or perhaps they are hedging their butterfly bets. How many eggs do they expect to survive?

7.

My parents are not butterflies. Social climbing, after all, is not the same as social butterflying. They did what was fitting, not what was flitting. Neither could be said to have *flitted about.*

They were not careless, and yet. They were not restless, and yet. Somehow all their eggs ended up in one basket.

I was not the egg they were expecting: not before my metamorphosis, not after. But I was the solitary egg that survived.

8.

When I begin to dance at the Southwest Community Center, I am disappointed by how much of ballet involves standing beside the barre or sitting on the floor. Where are the great sweeps and leaps across the stage? Where are the ceaseless pirouettes that transform the ballerina into a wind-up doll?

Arranged by height, I am the one who looms, casting a shadow from the back of the room. Later, we come forward and link arms and face the mirror, then fold ourselves into little flowers. Now I am the gladiolus in a field of marigolds, towering, ever at risk of toppling.

Miss Erika pats our heads as she takes the roll—our cue to blossom. One at a time, we rise to our feet without using our hands. This I cannot do.

Seated again, we press the soles of our stiff pink slippers together—all but Edgars, whose slippers are black because he is a boy. "Be the beautiful butterflies I know that you are!" Miss Erika waves her hands like magic. The girls flutter their legs; the boy flutters his legs. Everyone, it seems, can be beautiful.

"Butterfly lands on a flower!" the teacher smiles, and we bring our knees all the way up to our chins. This I can do.

"Butterfly spreads its wings!" We bring our knees all the way down to the floor. But mine pop up again—they will not stay low, even when Miss Erika lays her hands upon them.

"Soften," she whispers. "We don't force our way into things. We soften."

In my bedroom at home, I sit with books on my knees, pleased by the fine heft of them, yet my body will not submit.

I am a butterfly at half-mast. Muscles coiled like springs. I have not unwound yet.

9.

It's 1987, and people are marching on the nation's capital. Spectators estimate half a million, dense and gleaming with potential. They raise their flags like brightly colored wings.

On this day, the AIDS Memorial Quilt is finally unfolded. On this day, the first community wedding for same-sex couples is performed.

WE ARE EVERYWHERE! one banner reads. Another: OUR FIGHT HAS JUST BEGUN. And—like the game I am likely playing at just this moment—another: COME OUT, COME OUT, WHEREVER YOU ARE!

But I hide so well, crouched in the small room with the Christmas tree and its ornaments, deep beneath the basement stairs. No one believes I can fit there. My parents search and search, turning frantic toward the end, shouting my name. Somehow they miss me every time.

10.

It's 1987, and an article called "A Note on the Apparent Lowering of Moral Standards in the Lepidoptera" has just been published. The article begins:

It is a sad sign of our times that the National newspapers are all too often packed with the lurid details of declining moral standards and horrific sexual offences committed by our fellow Homo sapiens; *perhaps it is also a sign of the times that the entomological literature appears of late to be heading in a similar direction. I published a short note on aberrant sexual behavior in butterflies observed on Mount Kenya in 1983 (Tennet: 1984) and recently returned home from a spell abroad to find similar behavior recorded in no less than three of the latest issues of different entomological journals (Hobbs: 1986, Knill-Jones: 1986, Winter: 1985). Unfortunately, I'm afraid there's more:—*

11.

It's 1987, second grade, and I am still ahistorical. My world has a perforated edge.

Of note this year: my first male teacher, the only man to stand on the yellow line and corral us all at the end of recess. No whistle. He beckons and bellows. His presence violates a trust I cannot name.

My mother, who is also a teacher, says, "Mr. Whited isn't any different from Edgars in ballet class. It's only natural that some men will be dancers and some men will be teachers."

But that word again, and why is it not *natural* that I want to wear boxing gloves, big and red as tulips; that I want to learn how to mow the lawn instead of arranging the flowers?

She must mean the dancing when she says: "After all, who is going to lift the women up?"

On the last day of school, Mr. Whited sets our report cards in the chalk tray, instructs us each to come to the front of the room.

The boys go first and are told to practice their handshakes: "Make it firm," he says, "or there'll be consequences." Some boys have to shake three times before they can take their grades and leave. "No sissies in my class" follows them out the door.

Then, scratching his beard as though he's just thought of it now: "From the young ladies, a kiss will be required." Wagging his fat white finger: "No butterfly kisses either."

One by one, I watch my classmates disappear, like nectar draining from a cup. He is sipping us through a straw. He is smirking.

When it's my turn, I reach for the card. "Not so fast. What are you forgetting?" I try to shake his hand, try to turn one cheek, then the other. But Mr. Whited finds my mouth and forces his whiskered lips upon it.

12.
The red dictionary in my grandmother's closet drapes over my knees like a skirt. The pages are deckle-edged. They form an uneven hem.

We keep the dictionary here with the board games, but sometimes I sit on the ledge for company and partially close the door. When I hold a book of any size on my lap, I can feel the words vibrating inside. Not once have I doubted that language is alive.

Sometimes I look up words I already know, like flipping through a family album. I miss their faces as much as I miss their sounds.

Chrysalis turns the tongue into a razor, sharp before soft: a knife passing through bread first, then through butter. *Cocoon*, which is not a synonym, reminds me of calling into a deep cave and listening for the echo.

The cocoon is something larvae build to protect themselves: a structure, not unlike this closet, which humans have carved into a wall.

The chrysalis is something larvae become: a hardening that happens as they enter their pupal stage. Most butterflies-to-be, with few exceptions, do not build cocoons. Most moths-to-be, with few exceptions, do.

Above my head, the coats—some wrapped in cellophane—billow softly. Sometimes a restless sleeve reaches down to pat my head.

Little flower, it almost says.

13.
So much gashed skin among my peers in these years, so many fleeting sutures.

It becomes a point of pride with certain boys. "Twenty stitches!" Carl brags upon returning to class. He wants to scare me, to get my goat: "Did you know they sew you up with a real needle? Then, you have to go back so they can cut out the thread."

Though clumsy, I am not fragile. I trip over laces. I fall out of trees. My mother worries most about my teeth—"those nice straight teeth that aren't going to need braces, thank God!" She reminds me to close my mouth whenever plummeting toward the ground.

In all my youth, the most I will ever require are a few butterfly stitches when the gash at my elbow or knee widens beyond the size of the standard Curad. These are not really stitches at all but thin white bandages that open like wings.

"Better than stitches," my mother says, "because they lessen the likelihood of scarring." To scar is to lessen the possibility of beauty, you see, or to reduce a present beauty exponentially.

Once, I hear the school nurse call them "butterfly closures" while reaching inside her bright red box. The world likewise demands closure. Doors closed, wounds closed, mouths closed, legs closed—everywhere besides ballet class. And then how persistently they will not open!

14.
My mother never speaks of miscarriages. My mother never speaks of cancer. There were only the long years of *trying*, of *waiting*—then the promise of one new life.

Childhood is larval, is wingless, is worm-like. We wriggle. We are afraid of where our growth will lead us, the resemblances yet to come. We are also afraid of not resembling enough.

Once, my mother suggested they might have brought home the wrong child from the hospital. "But that only happens in movies," she laughed.

Both of us lingered in the moment's cocoon. We ate our way deep into disappointment.

15.

Always, I was a hungry child. Even a *very* hungry child. When babysitting, I read to other children, put them to bed, then raided their parents' pantry and fridge. Just a few years older, but somehow old enough to stay up late and alone.

Taylor and Alex wanted to hear *The Very Hungry Caterpillar* every time I came. They could recite it page by page. A clever book: primer for counting with pictures that beguile. Teaches children how quantities add up; the dangers, too, of overindulgence.

It really has nothing to do with butterflies.

The caterpillar eats everything in sight: first an apple, then two pears, three plums, four strawberries, five oranges—after that, a terrible bellyache.

Aunt Linda has gone on a diet like this but with grapefruits. Only grapefruits. So many grapefruits she could fill a wheelbarrow. She never gets full, and she never drops weight. Still, she never blames the grapefruits for her unchanging fate.

Later, the caterpillar eats a giant green leaf and spins himself a lovely cocoon.

While the children sleep, I pop lids on sealed jars, puncture packages with butter knives. I devour Spanish olives, strings of cheese, and pepperoni sticks. Everything I never get at home. Juice boxes galore. My belly doesn't hurt. The space inside me feels infinite.

In the bathroom, this family keeps a box of Cheerios. The boys toss them in the toilet before they take a whiz. "For target practice," their mother says, as if this is commonplace. Perhaps it is. I'm beguiled by that big yellow box and heart-shaped bowl, something wholesome, even *natural*, about a name brand. Fistful by fistful, I eat my way through to the other side.

16.

Now it's 1991, and everywhere I see the girl with the butterfly covering her mouth. Or is it a moth? Maybe a moth. Moth-mouth. Even the words touch each other softly.

I know I'm supposed to notice whether the antennae are feathery or have bulbs at the ends. I'm supposed to spot the frenulum or the absence thereof.

But all I can think about are her hidden lips: how I would like to be the creature that alights there, obscuring them. How the dark heat of her missing mouth is a secret I would like to enter.

17.

On winter weekends, we head for the mountains to Snoqualmie Pass and the hot pursuit of powder.

Somehow, on skis, I am graceful. In this way, I take after my mother. First, we race each other down the mountain. Then, on smaller slopes, we practice our royal Christies, also known as butterfly turns: extend the leg, arch the back, shift the weight, and glide.

"Beautiful, like a butterfly!" My father stands at a distance, whistles and waves.

It turns out I am good in the cold, smooth and efficient. Something about bundling, I suspect: the way no one can see the contours of my body through the puffed parka, the sagging bibs.

My instructor John says I have real promise with the slalom race. When he takes me up on the chairlift, I think he is going to tell me that I won. He is likely still a teenager: soft, clean-shaven face; sleek ear muffs instead of the usual pom-pom cap; eyes that are green in some lights and brown in others.

My mother has suggested to me that I should consider liking John. This is a project, similar to shuffling cards, making a place for him in my mind. I think maybe I will like John or that I do already, which explains why my palms moisten inside my Gore-Tex gloves when he offers me a Tic Tac.

I tug hard at the fingers of my glove with my teeth, exposing one hand, upturned. As he shakes the orange pellets from their plastic box, John says, "Look, I hate to break this to you, but you missed a gate out there." One Tic

Tac, two Tic Tacs, three. "On the course, you had the best time of anyone, but because of that gate, you were . . . disqualified."

18.

For many years, I feed my hunger. It is such an insistent question, and food seems the only reasonable reply.

Then comes the year when I begin to fear my hunger. A cousin sees me in a hot tub, makes a squiggle with her hand. "Not a straight line anymore, are you?" My heartbeat everywhere but where it belongs.

French bikinis are in vogue now: still a one-piece swimsuit, but with the belly cut out, an absent round of fabric and a new place to burn. Even the boys I babysit can't unglue their eyes from *Baywatch*. Though I am twelve, someone has bought me a subscription to *Seventeen*.

When I learn to love the hunger at last, to cradle it the way you would a hatchling, butterflies appear everywhere on my body: butterfly of the clavicles, butterfly of the sharp blades in my back, butterfly of the pelvis that carries me through the world.

And what do you call a group of butterflies? It's so obvious we think we must be wrong. *A flutter.*

19.

In 1992, my parents set the VCR to record *The Silence of the Lambs*. "It won so many Oscars," they say. "We figured we should see what all the fuss is about."

Later, when they leave for outlet shopping, I dim the lights and chew my nails. This is the first R-rated movie I have ever seen. Even edited for television, it's dangerous, elicit: a threshold I cannot uncross.

There is also the matter of this recurrent, prickly feeling when I recall the movie posters—*moth-mouth*—and imagine what the tape might contain.

Buffalo Bill is frightening, of course, the way he selects his victims by size. There are no fourteens in my closet yet, but what if it's true and I'm not done growing? When I was young, the pediatrician told my parents it was reasonable to expect me to reach six feet.

"You're not big!" My mother is always somewhere insisting. "Just tall!" Yet she doesn't seem to mind that I am shrinking—the skin ever tighter around my bones, my soft body hardening into chrysalis.

Afterward, my friend April whispers into the phone: "What did you think? Is it as scary as everyone says?"

"Yes," I reply, but I can't tell her everything. Instead, I explain in great detail about the exotic pupa the killer places inside each woman's throat—a symbol that he, too, is undergoing metamorphosis; that he, like the moth, will be reborn.

What I don't think but feel is desire: desire like a terrible bellyache, but sharper, sharper even than the sewing scissors my mother keeps beyond my reach.

I want to be close to Clarice, closer than the screen will permit, closer than I have ever been to any woman before.

How untenable this all sounds, impossible as a suit made of other people's skin. I can never explain the tug of it—not to April, not to anyone. For if I said, "I want to be inside a woman's body," what would prevent her from saying that most obvious thing: "But Julie—you already are."

20.
I was in Morocco recently and spent some time in and around Oukaimeden in the High Atlas Mountains south of Marrakech. On the 11th of June 1986 I was lucky enough to stumble upon a thriving colony of Cyaniris semiargus maroccana *just emerging in some long grass at ca. 2600 metres. Having taken some photographs I observed a cluster of four males flying closely around what I assumed to be a freshly emerged female sitting with her wings closed low down in the grass. Wanting photographs of a pair in cop I waited to see which, if any, of the males would be the successful suitor but soon realised that the object of their attention and affections was also a male. The attendant males vied with one another and each was curving his abdomen in a frantic attempt to make contact with the abdomen of the emerging male. The latter did not respond but was unable to escape as its wings were still soft. It laboriously made its way up the grass stem and was much buffeted by the others en route.*
                                                                    —Ibid.

21.
I keep thinking about the word *model*. There are model houses, model airplanes, model trains. *What are they meant to do, these models?* Show us the

nature of the thing: a perfect, smaller version of it? Not long ago, I learned the word *epitome*, and soon thereafter, *paragon*. Models are epitomes, paragons. They are the perfect, smaller versions of women, I conclude.

Krissy Taylor is six feet tall, one inch taller than her sister Niki. They appear together on the cover of *Seventeen*: slender flowers with bodies long as stems. *Wispy, willowy*, the commentators say. I am as thin as I will ever be, willowy in a way I cannot stay. At just this moment, I can feel my own flesh stretching, the way a leaf is sometimes added to a table.

In her backyard, April and I mimic the sisters' photo shoot. We find holey denim, sheer half-shirts, puka shells. We learn to hunch our shoulders and draw our stomachs in so that our limbs dangle like oversized clothes.

In one picture, we notice a butterfly painted on Krissy's cheek, but sadly we cannot replicate the image. Later, we read how her ankle bears a permanent butterfly tattoo. When I call about getting one, the man laughs into the phone. "Butterfly. Sure. How original!" Then, he changes his tone. "But if you're not eighteen, be sure to bring a parent or guardian."

22.

Always, my mother tells me how it will be when I fall in love: "You'll meet a man—maybe at work, maybe in medical school. He'll be tall, of course, because you're tall, and very handsome. And when you meet this man, you'll *know*."

"But what will I know exactly?"

"That he's *The One!*" My mother clasps her hands and bats her eyes dramatically.

Doubtful still, I press her: "But what if I don't ever meet a man like that?"

"Of course you will! It's only *natural*." Natural as a name brand, natural as a Hallmark card with two silhouettes—his broad shoulders, her narrow waist—strolling arm in arm along the shore.

"When you feel the butterflies," my mother instructs, "notice who put them there."

23.

The situation became even more strange when a fresh female came to rest with her wings open on a grass stem no more than a foot away. One of the four males approached her, she immediately raised her abdomen and vibrated her wings but after a very cursory examination the male returned to the pack and continued forcing his attentions on his fellow. During the next hour or so I saw a further three groups of males, one of which contained eight individuals, behaving in a similar manner towards fresh males whose wings were not yet dry.

—Ibid.

24.

There is something more ambitious about the way I exercise in 1994—something you might call punishing. I swim lap after lap, sometimes whole lengths of the butterfly kick, arms at my sides, cap so tight on my scalp even my thoughts are compressed.

In the locker room, a girl from the visiting swim team tells me I look like a sperm on a mission. "You're going to get that egg for sure!" she laughs, and some of the other girls join her. After that, I leave my curls loose, despite the green chlorine streaks in my hair.

At home, I work out with Cindy Crawford every day. When my father passes through the basement, he says, "Hey, she has a beauty mark above her lip just like you!"

Unlike me, Cindy Crawford drinks Evian water and has a personal trainer named Radu. Unlike me, she is married to a movie star with whom she'll soon take out a full-page ad in *The Times of London*: "We are heterosexual and monogamous and take our commitment to each other very seriously." My parents wonder what they are hiding, what they are trying to prove.

For all the crunches and leg lifts and lunges and squats, the best part about the Crawford workout is the weights. Here is a supermodel telling me to be strong, urging me to become more "defined." *What else have I been seeking but definition?*

Hardest to perform are the butterflies, though: Clasp the weights in front, keep the knees soft, don't use momentum. From the strength of your shoulders alone, raise your arms, spread them wide, then lower and repeat this motion. When my mother passes through the basement, she says, "Be careful you don't end up bulky like a man."

The next year, I no longer fit into any of my clothes. *Having emerged from its chrysalis, a butterfly usually sits on the empty shell in order to expand its wings.*

My biceps strain visibly against the tight ribbed knit. My quads threaten the seams of every skirt, even the pleated Tartan plaid. *Although tempting to call this period the metamorphosis, transition to adulthood is not yet complete.* My mother weeps in line at T.J. Maxx, mourning how big I have gotten.

The next year, Cindy Crawford files for divorce. My parents shake their heads and sigh.

25.
We are all girls at my high school, which the nuns say prevents temptation. No boys around to distract us from our studies. No boys to fill our bellies with those pesky butterflies.

There is one male teacher in the whole school—not a monk or even a priest—just layman Mr. Nowak, who teaches Chemistry. A single man teaching teenaged girls about chemistry, six periods a day, every day. Why am I the only one who finds this funny?

Before each lab, Mr. Nowak wheels out the green portable shower that looks like a recycling bin with nozzles and a drain. "Ladies, you know the drill. Pull your hair back. Put your goggles on. But if any part of you should catch fire, you jump right inside this bad boy and turn the water on full blast."

The joke's on him, though: We are smoldering already, molten as any molting thing.

26.
In English class, we are all girls assigned to read only poems by men. They're long-dead men, so we're unlikely to lust after any of them, except perhaps edgy Andrew Marvell.

"The worms are going to eat her corpse anyway," someone self-righteous says. "What does it matter about her cooch?"

But it does matter. We haven't decided yet whether our power rests in preservation of that deep cocoon, or whether power is always an act of emergence: stripping down, splaying wide, bearing all. (There is *closure*, on one hand—what the nuns have chosen; there is, on the other, *eclosure*.) "Don't you sometimes wish you could just *whip it out*? That you had something to whip out?" someone thoughtful says.

I nod. *Notice where the butterflies come from.* How I love the lilt of another girl's voice. How I love the learned silence in every girl's throat and the way she emerges through sound.

One day Sister Mary Annette hands us a photostat of George Herbert's "Easter Wings." She asks me to read it aloud:

> *My tender age in sorrow did beginne*
> *And still with sicknesses and shame.*
> *Thou didst so punish sinne,*
> *That I became*
> *Most thinne.*

On these lines, I linger. I underline the most familiar words: *Sorrow. Shame. Sinne. Thinne.*

"Why is the shape of this poem significant?" Sister presses. "Why does Herbert arrange the two stanzas as butterfly wings?"

While someone loquacious is speaking, I watch Sister's shadow sweep across the floor and then descend. She lifts the pencil out of my hand and turns it over, erasing the wrong thing I have done.

27.
Males on the emergence ground outnumbered females by about five to one although the latter sex were still common. The females habitually rested with their wings open and were often visited fleetingly by passing males, however, I did not see any females being 'pestered.' The time was about midday.
—Ibid.

28.
"Do you think being gay is a sin?" I ask my friend April—who goes to school with boys, who dates one of them, who may be a little distracted.

"I don't think so. I mean, how can a *person* be a sin?" She is dusting her eyelids with potent pastels, then swirling the colors together.

"That's a good point, and I totally agree, but in Catholic school—you hear things, you know. There's a lot of paranoia about it."

"Probably because people already think all those nuns and priests are gay.

Who knows? Maybe they are. But it's not really the *being* that's the problem, is it? They're just not supposed to act on it."

"Act on it?"

"Like—*do gay things.*"

Now the seashell phone on her nightstand is ringing. "Oh my God, what if it's Ryan?" April seizes my hand. I watch as her cheeks auto-rouge, as her chin starts to quiver. The pulse in her temple visibly throbs.

This is it, I think, what they mean by *aflutter*, the body so honest it must be believed. "Oh my God, Julie! How do I look?"

29.

It's 1997, and Ellen DeGeneres has just appeared on the cover of *TIME*. The caption reads, in the same red print as caution labels, as strike-through symbols on No Smoking signs: "Yep, I'm Gay."

I don't recognize this woman, but I won't lie; I'm intrigued. I see her face beaming back at me from the supermarket checkout line. It's too risky to buy the magazine of course, but when I search for it at school, I find that single issue missing from the well-stocked Periodicals section.

Perhaps in some subliminal way, I understand how ground-breaking this moment is. I am about to graduate from high school after all. I am about to leave for college. Yet no one I know, and no one I can imagine meeting, has ever—*would ever*—admit such a thing—"Yep, I'm gay"—let alone so casually, as though it were a mere aside.

And there's something else, something that troubles me about this cover: Despite the stranger's warm demeanor, her let's-talk-about-it-over-coffee smile, and the promised exclusive, "Ellen DeGeneres explains why she's coming out," it's the fact that she's squatting, nearly down on one knee, within the magazine's signature red border. *How can I not see a box there?* How can I not see a woman cordoned off, set apart, in submissive posture—beckoning, reassuring the hesitant reader that she's tame, or has been tamed, that she won't bite.

Come see the lesbian! the caption might have read.

I begin to shudder a little, like the first time I saw a butterfly displayed—animal no longer, artifact thereafter—wings pinned, body preserved under glass. A stand-in for the creature it once had been.

30.

It's 1997, and Christian singer-songwriter Bob Carlisle has just appeared on *Oprah* to perform his hit song, "Butterfly Kisses," written for his daughter Brooke. Summoned for mandatory family time, I sit with a rigid spine between my parents. I listen to the lyrics and parse them with my mind:

> *There's two things I know for sure:*
> *She was sent here from heaven*
> *And she's daddy's little girl.*

Was no one else troubled by this commonplace notion of daughter as angel, daughter as belonging to her dad?

By the second verse, she's "*sweet 16*," wearing "*perfume and makeup*" instead of "*ribbons and curls*." My mother mutters how it must be nice—"he has a daughter who actually takes pride in herself!" My father fishes a handkerchief out of his pocket and gingerly wipes his eyes; by the bridge, both my parents are sobbing. I'm embarrassed for them. The camera sweeps Oprah's audience as women—it is mostly women—cover their faces, rock and keen. When I look down at my lap, I see how my fists are clenched, how they mirror a fist I can feel forming inside.

Mind you, Brooke is my age. She looks as wholesome and wannabe as every girl I know: lips glossed, eyes lined, small diamond studs in her ears. She hasn't even left home, let alone married anyone, so the song's climactic verse is pure fantasia: a father conjuring the only outcome he can imagine for his female child.

Now my father passes his handkerchief to my mother, drapes his arm across my shoulder, and pulls me close. The song isn't finished yet, but I shrug myself free and spring to my feet. "This song is disgusting!" I shout—*at whom?* Oprah? Brooke? My stunned parents? The crooner himself, eyes closed as he leans into the mic and strums his sentimental guitar?

"This song makes me want to throw up on my shoes!"

"Julie!"

"No, this song makes me want to throw up on *his* shoes!"

"Julie!"

"What if she doesn't want to marry *anyone?* And God forbid if she doesn't want to change her name!"

I bolt up the stairs, but his voice follows me through the vents. I am plugging my ears, which are filled with an ominous beeping, but still I hear him. The heat in my face, the heartbeat in transit, the volume that won't stop rising.

On my birthday, I unwrap a copy of Bob Carlisle's *Shades of Grace*. It is one of only three CDs I own, one of only three to take for college. On the shrink-wrapped cover: an iridescent green swallowtail, its wingspan greater than the case. Inside the card: "We're praying for you! Love, Mom & Dad"

31.

It's 1997, and the University is a dictionary. Students live inside it. We are some of the terms we seek to define, but by no means all of them. Plump words fall at our feet. They roll down the aisles of lecture halls; they split open on seminar tables.

Collected: *Paradigm*, meaning a typical example or pattern of something; a model. It's a *dime*, not a *dig 'em*, but I'm tricked time and again by the silent *g*. (Or perhaps I am the silent *g*, a hidden presence that precipitates a *paradigm shift*.)

Collected: *Phantasmagoria*, meaning a series of real or imaginary images like those seen in a dream; derived from a mode of theater in which frightening specters were projected onto walls or semi-transparent screens. (I try it in a sentence: *My family's paradigm involves repressing phantasmagoria through prayer.*)

Collected: *Ally*, meaning to side with or lend support to a particular group or cause, or a person who forges such an alliance. I enlarge my paradigm to include an alliance with the LGBT community. (I wear blue jeans on National Coming Out Day. I stand beside a giant closet made of cardboard while other students gleefully leap through the door.)

Corollary: *Aposematism*, meaning the display of colors and patterns that warn predators the potential prey is unpalatable, toxic, or dangerous. Certain aposematic butterflies deter birds who have previously sampled those presenting the same visual paradigm. (My mother laments: "No boy is ever going to ask you out if you wrap yourself in rainbows!")

32.
But a boy does. And then another boy. And later even a man.

The boys are shy about their bodies. In this way, they resemble girls I have known and girls I have been. I feel an acute tenderness toward them, which for years I will struggle to transmute into desire. (Longing, I learn, has an infinite ambit, while lust is more particular than a needle's eye.)

For now, I blush when I gaze at them: boys with lank, hairless chests, their belts cinched over narrow hips, their legs long and bristled. What strange creatures—half-feminine, half-foreign. Notice the protruding fruit of the larynx, the deep sockets under the shoulders, the bright button of each wrist bone. I am as curious as a cartographer, summoned to map an uninhabitable landscape.

When a boy stretches out on the dorm room floor, I'm astonished by his rib cage—that huge butterfly rising out of his flesh—followed by the seismic flutter that accompanies every breath. He sighs and tosses his limbs.

This same boy will soon apologize for hardening against me as we dance: his chrysalis, his act of transformation. "I can't help it," he pleads, ears turning red. "I don't expect you to do anything about it."

I like him best when he is softest, when our bodies are mute so our voices can chatter. Then I feel him changing again, the sudden growth and upward thrust, his eyes caught between appetite and embarrassment.

"Little flower," I might have said.

33.
The man is different. He is older by a decade, unequivocal about his physicality. His body is more body than mine—bigger, stronger, surer in its footing, more fluent in its pleasure. I fumble. I pose. I listen for the buzzer that says we're done. I drop the butterflies back in his belly; I recede into mind.

Once, he reads me a poem he thinks I will love by Nabokov called "On Discovering a Butterfly": "I found it and I named it [...] thus became godfather to an insect and its first describer."

"Is this how you think of me?" I blurt, midway through. "As your little discovery on a pin?"

His dark eyes darken. "Why can't this just be a poem about a butterfly? Why is everything always a metaphor with you?"

I have stopped apologizing for my body—how it looks or doesn't look, how it moves or doesn't move. This is progress. Sometimes, though, I use my body to apologize for other things. This is less progressive, I realize.

He comes, he comes, he comes—and in the end, I go.

34.

The body carries experience. This we know. The body holds and hides experience. This we know also. But language often reveals what we have cloaked most carefully, exposing us—*eclosing* us—while we believe ourselves contained.

Consider this artifact, composed after kissing a boy in the college square— after being seen doing so—which was essential to my enterprise. Then back to my little room with the metal desk, the lamp that made a small white halo on my paper, writing.

Only one copy still extant after hand-delivering the poem to the girl—my friend from English class. She hardly knew what to say. Can you blame her?

Butterfly Girl

I think I have fallen in love
          the way artists do   with a subject
that day-week-month-year after   when it is no longer enough
                    to contemplate a face or simulate a grace of motion
          I must know you
And it is not like it is with men, when I think I must beautify myself
          for their indulgence,   or they must intellectualize themselves
                    for my compliance
                              No, it is the way women love each other
               Our Eve-love salt of the earth snowy womb of heaven
     alone in the wilderness kind of Love   that draws me in
                              and maybe you too
                    although in this light it's hard to say
And what do I want?   nothing   that's the most beautiful part
          That it's enough to have your heat wave of a heart directed at me

every once and a while,
concentrated intense
precipitating poems like ripe wordless plums
and promises that, if they ever fell
from your lips

would   *forever*
be   ,   *mind*
caught   *my*
in   *of*
the   net

I lay awake and will not sleep a long time because of you

Years from now, Angie will ask, incredulous: "And you didn't mean this as a coming-out poem?"

"No," I will tell her. "I thought I was staying in."

35.

The Counting Crows warbled through my Walkman for years—on a furtively copied cassette with ribbons I tightened by pencil tip—*Snap her up in a butterfly net. Pin her down on a photograph album.*

How I loved the angst and equivocation transmitted through Duritz's voice, especially in this song, "Anna Begins." These lines in particular: how they pierced me, then flung me away, forgotten until the next rewind/re-play, when I was stunned all over again.

I read philosophy for years, hoping to become wise, but was mostly disappointed by the lack of imagery accompanying the thinkers' arguments. As a consequence, I cherished this sensory thought-puzzle from Zhuangzi:

I dreamed I was a butterfly, flitting around in the sky; then I awoke. Now I wonder: Am I a man who dreamt of being a butterfly, or am I a butterfly dreaming I am a man?

Then this, from Annie Dillard's *An American Childhood*, perhaps my most important literary encounter:

The mason jar sat on the teacher's desk; the big moth emerged inside it. The moth had clawed a hole in its hot cocoon and crawled out, as if agonizingly, over the course of an hour, one leg at a time; we children watched around the desk, transfixed. After it emerged, the wet, mashed thing turned around walking on the green jar's bottom, then painstakingly climbed the twig with which the jar was furnished.

There, at the twig's top, the moth shook its sodden clumps of wings. When it spread those wings—those beautiful wings—blood would fill their veins, and the birth fluids on the wings' frail sheets would harden to make them tough as sails. But the moth could not spread its wide wings at all; the jar was too small. The wings could not fill, so they hardened while they were still crumpled from the cocoon.

It was a mistake. A smaller moth could have easily spread its wings inside that jar, but not a moth as big as the Polyphemus that emerged. No one meant any harm, yet harm would inevitably follow.

Even now, retyping this passage, I cry for the creature that did not know its potential had been limited, its lifespan cut short by accident, and for the way Dillard describes its bittersweet release from the jar:

I knew that this particular moth, the big walking moth, could not travel more than a few more yards before a bird or a cat began to eat it, or a car ran over it. Nevertheless, it was crawling with what seemed wonderful vigor, as if, I thought at the time, it was still excited from being born. I watched it go till the bell rang and I had to go in. I have told this story before, and may yet tell it again, to lay the moth's ghost, for I still see it crawl down the broad black driveway, and I still see its golden wing clumps heave.

36.

Consider two bildungsromane:

How does a plain old caterpillar become such a (   ) (   ) (   ) butterfly?

In the lepidopteran life cycle, a caterpillar emerges from a fertilized egg and devotes itself first to a period of voracious feeding. When the caterpillar (larva) has grown sufficiently strong, it attaches itself by a button of silk to the underside of a branch, stone, or other projecting surface. The caterpillar, now transformed into a pupa, remains attached to the silk pad by a hook-like process called cremaster. Most chrysalids hang head downward, but in certain families, the chrysalis is held in a more upright position by a silk girdle. Upon eclosure, the butterfly (imago) must dry and expand its wings, allowing them to harden adequately before first flight. Reflecting all the vivid hues of the rainbow, butterflies are remarkably diverse in size, wing-span, and phenotype. Some migrate significant distances and are equipped with a precise, natural compass to guide them.

How does a nice young lady become such a ( ) ( ) ( ) lesbian?

There is also great hunger and the need to grow strong. There is also a period of extreme confinement, during which she must bend her ear to the truest silence of her interior world (knowing place). She must learn to hear the unspoken as clearly as the spoken and sift them both. Ask any adolescent girl about *pupa*—from the Latin, meaning "doll." She was always already a pupa, and if she is not careful, she will remain one the rest of her life. Yes, there is much to master. Yes, her head will often hang downward, shamed by the ways she is made to feel too much and too little at once (paradox). In certain families, the silk girdle is especially tight. She will have to do more than rip it—she will have to *rend it unrecognizable*—in order to emerge. These adults are likewise remarkably diverse in their hues, sizes, and desires. Ask any human woman about the *imago*, which also means "an unconscious and idealized mental image of someone, which influences that person's behavior." She knows instinctively what you mean. Say *mother*. Say *teacher*. Say *Holy Mary, Mother of God*. Say *supermodel*. Say even *butterfly*—pretty and delicate and unobtrusive, the way she was taught to be. Say *wife*, and she'll see two images superimposed—a *husband* (general) and a *ring* (specific)—even if she doesn't want to see them. Queer variants in all species exist. Often, they must travel a greater distance from their first flowers. They, too, are equipped with a precise compass. Their migrations are natural.

37.
To set the reader's mind at rest I should also record that I subsequently observed a number of 'normal' pairs in cop; at least some [butterflies] had the further-ance of the colony at heart and the appearance of the colony next year is thereby assured.

> *Whatever next?!*

—Ibid.

38.
In 2002, I come upon "A Note on the Apparent Lowering of Moral Standards in the Lepidoptera"—*Was I reading this right? Immoral butterflies?*—

published a quarter-century prior in a scientific journal. The entomologist's seemingly genuine horror at having witnessed a group of male butterflies vying to "make contact with the abdomen of [an] emerging male" startles me at first, then leaves me doubled over my desk, laughing.

My beloved steps into the living room of our small apartment to ask what is happening, and I try to explain: "From his tone, it's as if these predatory gay butterflies are all smoking in a dark alley—wearing fishnets under their trenchcoats, no less—just waiting to pounce on the unassuming male youth who takes the trash out of the nightclub kitchen. The article even mentions that his wings were not yet dry. *Such innocence!*"

"You should write that down," Angie says, and so I do.

During this time, I have been reading about butterflies because for many months I've suffered a recurring dream that I am choking on one, and when I awake, the sensation persists. I sit up, drenched in sweat, and I can feel—*I swear I can*—something fluttering inside my throat.

To the endocrinologist, I make a wan joke: "Some people complain of a frog in the throat, but mine has wings." Then, a nervous pun: "It feels like a Monarch in there—*a king with wings!*"

Dr. McAfee smiles. "Well, you know, everyone has a butterfly in their throat to begin. It's the thyroid gland." I don't know. She shows me a picture, and sure enough: "See? Shaped just like a butterfly. Yours, for reasons we don't yet understand, has begun to swell and distend." She touches my neck gently. "Your windpipe and your voicebox are both right here, so trouble with the thyroid can affect them as well."

Before surgery, my first time going under the knife, my beloved stands beside my hospital bed and suggests we try a different phrase.

"I think the technical name is *thyroidectomy*. Does that sound any less torturous?" I ask.

"Slightly." Her eyes are so blue I can see the ocean in them.

"You know, I'd like to write about that strange article, but I think I need to find out more about the *lesbian* Lepidoptera scene."

We try to keep it light. Angie holds my hand. I can feel how cold her fingers are, though also dry, which suggests she hates this occasion but trusts the outcome will be fine. I notice also the pretty moons of her nail beds, the white crescents rising.

"Well, if that scientist was scandalized by males *in cop*," she says, "there's a good chance he'll be titillated by the ladies."

"Or he'll think they're all just friends—just some nice girl-butterflies at a nectar klatsch!"

We are chuckling when the surgeon comes in. "That's what I like to see," he grins. "Good spirits." He also believes, despite clarification, that we are friends and only friends.

After Angie leaves the room, this surgeon explains the operation to me one last time. *It's really true*, I marvel. *He's going to reach inside my body and lift a butterfly out.*

His last words dangle over me like a mobile above a crib: "I will do my very best not to nick a vocal cord. We on the surgical team are committed to preserving your voice."

Maybe I am ready for the butterfly, or the absence thereof. Or maybe there is no ready, only *ready or not, here it comes*. Not a *deflowering* exactly—but *de-winging* of a kind. Life without a vital organ? I hear Aunt Linda in a voiceover say, *That just isn't done!* I watch droplets of something translucent passing through a tube. *Tube* sounds more neutral than *vial*, which reminds me of *vile* and which I sometimes misspell. There will be a scar, surely. Will my mother ever see it? Do I care, one way or the other? I have already flown so far. Once a woman dreamed she was a butterfly—or maybe a butterfly dreamed she was a woman. *I will need my voice, though.* Can he hear me say that? My eyelids are fluttering now. A nurse says, "Don't fight it, dear." Goddamn that song "Butterfly Kisses," though it would make Angie laugh if I played it for her now. I love making Angie laugh. *I will need my voice, Sir!* I love Angie. Then, at last: I soften. I soften.

Notes

"Meditation 32"

The quote beginning "We're a little lost . . . " is from Carole Maso's lyric essay, "The Intercession of the Saints," first encountered in *The Next American Essay,* edited by John D'Agata and published by Graywolf Press in 2003.

The quote beginning "How shall we speak of love . . . " is from Mary Oliver's poem, "Work," from her book, *The Leaf and the Cloud*, published by Da Capo Press in 2000.

The quote beginning "I think I grow tensions . . . " is from Robert Creeley's poem, "The Flower," first published in the February 1966 issue of *Poetry* magazine and later in *The Collected Poems of Robert Creeley, 1945-1975* by University of California Press.

The quote beginning "[We] are the music while the music lasts" is from T.S. Eliot's book-length poem, *Four Quartets* ("The Dry Salvages"), published by Harcourt in 1943.

"Tremolo"

The Galway Kinnell poems referenced are "The Night" and "Rapture," first encountered in *Imperfect Thirst*, published by Ecco in 1994.

The quote beginning "Let me not to the marriage of true minds . . . " is from William Shakespeare's "Sonnet 116," first published in 1609.

The quote beginning "You're in love with my mind . . . " is from Sandra Cisneros's poem, "Full Moon and You're Not Here," first encountered in *Loose Woman*, published by Vintage in 1994.

The quote beginning "She will be all day, among strangers . . . " is from "Rapture" by Galway Kinnell.

The quote beginning "Wild nights - Wild nights! Were I with thee . . . " is from Emily Dickinson's poem "Wild nights - Wild nights! (269)," written in 1861 and published posthumously.

The line "him like the big folded wings of her" is from "The Night" by Galway Kinnell.

The line "Longing, we say, because desire is full of endless distances" is from "Meditation at Lagunitas" by Robert Hass, from his book *Praise*, published by Ecco in 1979. The poem is discussed further on subsequent pages.

The quote beginning "All those girls knew Petra was taking me home to fuck me . . . " is from Michelle Tea's memoir, *Valencia*, published by Seal Press in 2000.

The line "Do I dare disturb the universe?" is from T.S. Eliot's poem, "The Love Song of J. Alfred Prufrock," first published in the June 1915 issue of *Poetry* magazine.

The line "these mornings I wish books loved back" is from Sandra Cisneros's poem, "Bay Poem for Berkeley," first encountered in *Loose Woman*, published by Vintage in 1994.

The quote beginning "The world tells me I am its creature" is from Adrienne Rich's poem, "Splittings," from her book, *Collected Poems: 1950–2012*, published by W.W. Norton & Company in 2016.

"Still Life with Guns"

The lyric referenced is from Irving Berlin's "You Can't Get a Man with a Gun," written for the 1946 musical, *Annie Get Your Gun.*

The quote beginning "My plan was to get him to come with me . . . " is from Eli Sanders's article "The Shooter," published in the February 27, 2003 issue of *The Stranger*, Seattle's alternative weekly.

The lyrics referenced are from "Smackwater Jack," a song written by Gerry Goffin and Carole King, which appears on King's 1971 album, *Tapestry.*

The quote beginning "Pacific Lutheran University students call their campus 'the Lute Dome'. . . " is from the article "PLU music professor slain in campus shooting; suicidal gunman leaves 16-page note," co-authored by Ray Rivera, Keiko Morris, and Eli Sanders, published on May 18, 2001 in *The Seattle Times.*

The excerpt from "The Coroner's Photographs" by Brent Staples was first encountered in Staples's memoir, *Parallel Time: Growing Up in Black and White,* published by Pantheon Books in 1994.

"Meditation 35"

The quote beginning "the physical realities of our lives . . . " is from *This Bridge Called My Back: Writings by Radical Women of Color,* coedited by Gloria Anzaldúa and Cherríe L. Moraga and first published by Persephone Press in 1981.

The blurb referenced comes from Suzanne Paola, my mentor in the graduate program at Western Washington University. I have come to see her characterization of my writing as originating in the body as the highest form of praise.

"How Do You Like Them"

The lines "Call it an apple. Call this a test or a joke" are from Rae Armantrout's poem, "As We're Told," which I first encountered in *American Women Poets in the 21st Century: Where Lyric Meets Language,* edited by Claudia Rankine and Juliana Spahr and published by Wesleyan University Press in 2002.

The line "Later, though, Mother puts the apple into Snow White's hand, and then it's poison!" comes from the same Rae Armantrout poem.

The lines "ten thousand thousand," "Magnified apples appear and disappear, Stem end and blossom end, And every fleck of russet showing clear" and "For I have had too much Of apple-picking: I am overtired Of the great harvest I myself desired" are from Robert Frost's poem, "After Apple-Picking," first published in *North of Boston* in 1914 by David Nutt.

The lines "Carnal apple, Woman filled, burning moon, dark smell of seaweed, crush of mud and light, what secret knowledge is clasped between your pillars?" are from Pablo Neruda's poem "Carnal Apple, Woman Filled, Burning Moon," which I first encountered in *Full Woman, Fleshly Apple, Hot Moon: Selected Poems,* published in English and Spanish by Harper-Collins in 1997.

The line "It would take fire or breaking glass to tell them the poppy, the apple, and the vein" are from Jennifer Oakes's poem, "The Listener," first published in *Willow Springs,* Issue 44, June 1999.

The lines "I can see why a pinecone would wish to be an apple, but it is less obvious why an apple would want to be a pinecone" appear in Katerina Stoykova-Klemer's collection, *The Air around the Butterfly,* published in English and Bulgarian by Fakel Express in 2009.

The lines "Such tenderness, those afternoons and evenings, saying *blackberry, blackberry, blackberry*" appear in Robert Hass's poem, "Meditation at Lagunitas," first published in *Praise* by Ecco in 1979.

"Meditation 36"

The epigraph comes from Camille Rankine's poem, "Forecast," first published by the Academy of American Poets' *Poem-a-Day* series on September 1, 2015.

The lines "One morning in Orlando, Florida, I asked a group of college students—What would you be willing to give up to equalize the wealth in the world? [...] A car, the guy with the nose ring said, I don't have a car anyway" and "Would I give up dyeing my hair? That was a hard one. If I stopped dyeing my hair everyone would know that my golden hair is actually gray, and my long American youth would be over—and then what?" are from Marie Howe's prose-poem, "What We Would Give Up," from *The Kingdom of Ordinary Time,* published by W.W. Norton & Company in 2009.

"Prose & Cons: Considerations from a Woman with Two Genres"

My prose-poem "Y" was selected by guest judge Albert Goldbarth as cowinner (with Yerra Sugarman) of the 2004 Chicago Literary Award in Poetry. It was published by *Another Chicago Magazine, 44 + 45,* Spring 2005.

The sample found poems were originally posted by Karen Salyer McElmurray on her Facebook page. I used them in class as models for my students—and in this essay—with her gracious permission.

The textbook referenced is *The Practice of Creative Writing: A Guide for Students* by Heather Sellers, Second Edition, published by Bedford/St. Martin's in 2012.

The lines "Before I built a wall I'd ask to know What I was walling in or out And to whom I was like to give offence. Something there is that doesn't love a wall, That wants it down" and "Good fences make good neighbors" are from Robert Frost's poem, "Mending Wall," first published in *North of Boston* in 1914 by David Nutt.

I'm grateful to Dwight Tracey, Jr., Stephanie Diaz, and Crystal Falloon for their genre insights and for permitting me to share them in this essay.

The inscription *"For Julie—the woman with two genres! With deep admiration for your poems and nonfiction!!"* is from Denise Duhamel, which she included in my copy of *The Woman with Two Vaginas* (Salmon Run Press, 1994) and granted permission for me to include in this essay. Denise is one the two Very Famous Poets referenced in this essay. The other is my friend and colleague, Campbell McGrath.

"Meditation 38"

The epigraph comes from Dana Levin's poem, "Ars Poetica (cocoons)," from *Wedding Day*, published by Copper Canyon Press in 2005.

The song referenced is "(You Make Me Feel Like a) Natural Woman," written by Gerry Goffin and Jerry Wexler with music composed by Carole King. It was first released in 1967 as a single by Aretha Franklin and later recorded by Carole King in 1971.

The article referencing butterfly mating habits is *The Entomologist's Record and Journal of Variation*: "A Note on the Apparent Lowering of Moral Standards in the Lepidoptera" by W.J. Tennent, 1987.

The article referencing Cindy Crawford and Richard Gere appeared in *The Times of London,* May 7, 1994.

Notes

The lines "My tender age in sorrow did beginne And still with sicknesses and shame. Thou didst so punish sinne, That I became Most thinne" are from George Herbert's "Easter Wings," published in his posthumous collection, *The Temple*, in 1633.

The song referenced is "Butterfly Kisses," written by Bob Carlisle and Randy Thomas and appearing on Carlisle's album *Butterfly Kisses (Shades of Grace)*, released May 13, 1997.

The poem referenced is Vladimir Nabokov's "On Discovering a Butterfly," first published in *The Atlantic Monthly* in 1941.

The song lyrics referenced are from "Anna Begins," written and released by Counting Crows on their 1993 album, *August and Everything After*.

The lines referenced are from Annie Dillard's *An American Childhood*, first published by Harper & Row in 1987.

Acknowledgments

I'll always be grateful to Lia Purpura for her probing, instructive, and infinitely teachable lyric essay collections and thrilled that she selected this manuscript for the 2022 Autumn House Nonfiction Prize. I'm also grateful to the entire editorial team at Autumn House for guiding *Otherwise* to print, especially Christine Stroud and Devan Murphy, who provided immense and incisive feedback on multiple drafts and helped me realize my fullest vision for this book.

I wrote *Otherwise* throughout my thirties, but some touchstone figures from my life well precede that decade. Thank you to my enduring friends, Anna Rhodes and James Allen Hall, and to my formative mentors, Dana Anderson and Tom Campbell, both of whom inspired me to pursue writing and teaching as my twin vocations. The next great mentors—Suzanne Paola, Bruce Beasley, Brenda Miller, Catherine Fosl, and Annette Allen (may you rest in peace), propelled me further and further along the way.

In 2012, I was hired by the English department at Florida International University to teach creative nonfiction and poetry to undergraduate and graduate students. This experience has been, and continues to be, one of the greatest joys and most rewarding challenges of my life. I'm grateful for all I've learned from my students and colleagues, especially these incomparables: Denise Duhamel, John Dufresne, Cindy Chinelly, and Debra Dean.

Thank you to my chosen family—Kim, Matt, Evie, Nolan ("Super Hondo"), and Sam Striegel, a.k.a. my "Outlaws"—for more than twenty years of love, acceptance, and outstanding adventures together.

Thank you to my cousin, Laura Olsavsky—new friend, avid reader, and fellow writer, too. I'm so lucky you found me and thought to reach out!

Thank you most of all to Angie Griffin, my favorite person and brightest light.

Acknowledgments

~

Thank you to the editors of these journals for publishing these essays along the way:

"**Meditation 32**" was published by *Fourth Genre: Explorations in Nonfiction* in 2013.

"**Tremolo**" was published as a stand-alone chapbook and winner of the 2012 BLOOM Nonfiction Chapbook Prize, selected by guest judge Bernard Cooper.

"**Still Life with Guns**" was published by *Fourth Genre: Explorations in Nonfiction* in 2017 as a finalist for the Michael Steinberg Essay Prize.

"**Meditation 35,**" a finalist for the *Iowa Review* Nonfiction Prize and the *Crab Orchard Review* Nonfiction Prize, was published by *Crab Orchard Review* in 2015.

"**How Do You Like Them**" was published by *Seneca Review* in 2016.

"**Nine Innings**" was published by *Fugue* in 2015.

"**Meditation 36**" was selected by guest judge Michael Martone as the winner of the Thomas Wilhelmus Award in Creative Nonfiction and was published by *Southern Indiana Review* in 2016.

"**Prose & Cons: Considerations from a Woman with Two Genres**" was published by *Tupelo Quarterly* in 2014 as a finalist for the *Tupelo Quarterly* Prose Open Competition.

"**Meditation 38**" was published by *Colorado Review* in 2018.

NEW AND FORTHCOMING FROM AUTUMN HOUSE PRESS

Taking to Water by Jennifer Conlon
Winner of the 2022 Autumn House Poetry Prize, selected by Carl Phillips

◆

Discordant by Richard Hamilton
Winner of the 2022 CAAPP Book Prize, selected by Evie Shockley

◆

The Neorealist in Winter: Stories by Salvatore Pane
Winner of the 2022 Autumn House Fiction Prize, selected by Venita Blackburn

◆

Otherwise: Essays by Julie Marie Wade
Winner of the 2022 Autumn House Nonfiction Prize, selected by Lia Purpura

◆

Murmur by Cameron Barnett

◆

Ghost Man on Second by Erica Reid
Winner of the 2023 Donald Justice Poetry Prize, selected by Mark Jarman

◆

Half-Lives by Lynn Schmeidler
Winner of the 2023 Rising Writer Prize in Fiction, selected by Matt Bell

◆

Nest of Matches by Amie Whittemore

For our full catalog please visit: http://www.autumnhouse.org